Jon is an agile catalyst; helping organisations to produce improved bottom-line when adopting agile.

A Change Management expert for over thirty years, Jon believes in contextual agile. Rather than using one framework or set techniques, Jon introduces appropriate ways of agile working enabling organisations to achieve their strategic goals. For Jon, this contextual focus involves tailoring agile approaches and blending them with traditional techniques. For example; recently, Jon combined Benefits Management approaches with components from SAFe and Disciplined Agile. Consequently, Jon has a reputation as a pragmatist; for implementing new ways of working, which make a difference.

To my wife, Tatiana, for your inspiration, encouragement and support.
ты причина, по которой я живу

Dave Bardell, Alex Clark and Bob Phillips
with thanks for your professional mentoring
over many, many years!

Jon Ward

THE AGILE COACH'S COOKBOOK

THE PATHWAY TO BENEFICIAL AGILE

AUSTIN MACAULEY PUBLISHERS™

LONDON ∗ CAMBRIDGE ∗ NEW YORK ∗ SHARJAH

A CIP catalogue record for this title is available from the British Library.

ISBN 9781398402539 (Paperback)
ISBN 9781398402546 (ePub e-book)

www.austinmacauley.com

First Published (2021)
Austin Macauley Publishers Ltd
25 Canada Square
Canary Wharf
London
E14 5LQ

I want to thank Gustav Bjorkeroth, Alex Clark, Geof Ellingham, Alan Gedye, Kenny Grant, Dimitar Karaivanov, Richard Kok, Theresa McGouran, Phil Moore, Eileen Roden, Virpi Rowe, Emil Schnabel, Lindsay Scott and Tanya Ward, for their feedback and for the time that they invested in helping me to either prove tools and concepts or help me to write this book. I could not have done this without you.

Table of Contents

Introduction

Since the publication of the manifesto, agile, has been treated by some as if it is merely a process. It seems as if there is a widely held belief that once people are trained or certified, suddenly, they are agile! Why is it then that once trained, and agile is simple in context, that people struggle and organisations fail, to realise the anticipated benefits of an agile culture? Why is it so hard? What's missing? The answer appears to lie in the area of coaching, that is taking the theory the books and training then applying these concepts in the reality of real work, delivering solutions for customers.

Getting good results with agile seems relatively straightforward: form a cross-functional team, prioritise work items in the form of a backlog, concentrate on small batch sizes and flow, create a potentially shippable product or customer value in each iteration. *Et voilà*! No surprises for the reader here? However, getting results – genuinely great results, consistently from agile teams – is a little more complicated.

Realising results which consistently excite senior executives, requires a great team with good working practices and a supportive ecosystem. As in sports, great teams rarely simply happen. Like great athletes, great teams are coached, shaped, challenged and conditioned over time. A sports team aspiring towards greatness needs a coach: trained, experienced and competent in their craft. The same is true of their agile team counterparts.

Great agile coaches have a desire, a passion, to help people and teams go further than they ever went before. These coaches listen and also continually develop themselves so that they are real wizards in their craft.

This book is an attempt to place into the hands of agile coaches, the practitioners – a series of recipes, some tools and techniques which will help them in their quest to build agile capabilities in organisations. Once they have become an agile leader, agile coaches or consultants tend to operate at three levels; Team enablement where coaching is focused on a single team potentially as a Scrum

Master role or similar. Agile Coaching where a coach may be working with several teams in a programme or department. Or Enterprise Agile Coaching is a consulting activity where a coach is involved or leading an organisational transformation. All these levels require a different but incremental skill set, yet all have the foundation in the self-awareness and knowledge of personal limitations of an agile leader.

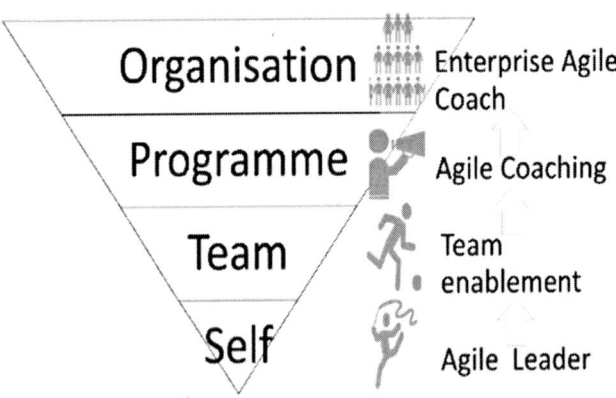

The layers of agile coaching

The book starts with outlining approaches, or recipes, which enable agile coaches to be leaders. Able to react to situations and to measure their success. It sets out some of the organisational prerequisites for agile adoption. Then it progresses through the coaching of teams to the programme level; covering the challenges of scaling agile for more substantial activities. The last section of the book is for Enterprise Agile Coaches or Consultants. It considers the planning, execution and control of agile transformational activities. It covers the identification and resolution of organisational anti-agile practices.

Formatted as a series of recipes for successful coaching. This book is not a definitive work; it's a minimum viable product; there will be further iterations. The contents are the result of working through several successful agile transformations and learning as I go.

With transformational success comes a sense of achievement which for many may become career-defining! This sense of lifetime achievement is real for me! I wish the reader the same sense of accomplishment and continued learning during their agile journey.

In working in several organisations and many teams, I have established a mantra which I share.

> *Agile without metrics is anarchy*
> *Agile without quality is pointless*

The goal of this cookbook is to give the agile coach; factors to consider, some recipes, some tools and some pointers towards success which include both metrics and quality.

How to Use This Guide

Much of what makes agile work – really work, are the beliefs, the values and the ecosystem in which the agile team operates. The beliefs centre on dissatisfaction with traditional ways of working and a certainty that better ways can always be found. The values focus on the treatment of human beings as skilled individuals who understand their craft. The ecosystem is the combination of training, processes and tools that enable agile teams to deliver solutions as efficiently as possible and the system which allows organisations to adapt to changing circumstances quickly. The combination of beliefs, values and ecosystem enable organisations through their agile teams to respond to the sudden shifts in market conditions, the development of game-changing technologies or the actions of competitors.

Most agile teams use Scrum or Kanban to deliver high-quality solutions quickly, but it is more, it's also about the quality of the solution. In producing results rapidly, agile can be complemented with established practices of project, programme and portfolio management, quality assurance and control and change management. While agile is comparatively new, the agile coach would be ill-advised to ignore all the wisdom embedded in these traditional approaches. Inevitably, therefore, in my view, the skilled agile practitioner, may use tools and techniques from as many sources as appropriate to support their activities. I firmly believe that obsessively using only agile methods is unnecessary and potentially career-limiting for a coach. Instead, I see that many of the practices used in traditional solution delivery have applicability and can also add value in an agile context.

The agile at scale frameworks place structure and functions on top of the roles, ceremonies and artefacts, of Scrum or Kanban, yet few places an appropriate, in my view, emphasis on the tools and techniques of quality at scale. Also, few scaled agile frameworks outline the importance of Agile Portfolio Management in creating organisational agility. I firmly believe that if the organisation requires a dynamic, agile capability; the ability to adapt, move quickly, to be responsive, then this agility is created by the portfolio management mechanisms, and not by agile team practices.

This book places an equal focus on the quality of the outcomes and the delivery process itself. In the transformation section, the scope is broadened to include the implications from agile for the organisational ecosystem and the portfolio management capability.

Some agilists suggest that the best way to achieve greater organisational agility is to train the agile mindset or culture. However, Craig Larman[i] who with Bas Vodde, is best known for formulating Large Scale Scrum (LeSS), says "Culture follows structure" and Edgar Schein,[ii] in a similar vein, it is the direct and indirect mechanisms employed within organisations which create a resultant organisational culture.

Direct mechanisms would include the way the organisation; rewards exemplary performance, forms opinions, how status is displayed and how it promotes individuals. Indirect mechanisms do not influence the organisational culture directly, yet they determine behaviour indirectly. These would include; the formal operating procedures, the statements summarising corporate identity, the organisational mission and vision statements, and the corporate rituals such as executive town halls, all-hands meetings and so on. It is the combination of these direct and indirect mechanisms which form the enterprise ecosystem and create organisational DNA.

Therefore, if as coaches as we alter the ways of working at the team and corporate level, we will also be changing the culture and introduce the agile mindset over time.

Much of effective agile coaching is like conducting an orchestra and relies upon the ability to identify impediments to the team and organisational performance. At the team level, this could be divisions of labour or individual incentives. At the enterprise level, typically this involves the portfolio mechanisms; how the money flows to activities, the operational controls over expense, how people are assigned to work, activities approved and how they are

The coach as conductor

supported once they are in-flight. In other words, culture is the result of the organisational processes, and the people are required to behave within it. The coach, therefore, needs to identify these cultural influences. Identify what is constraining team performance and directly address these challenges.

An agile transformation is about altering the existing organisational processes, introducing new behaviours and tools. It is about how the requirements for solutions are collected, specified, designed, then built and replaced. Consequently, this book not only looks at how the coach interacts with each team but also identifies how to identify and make changes to the organisational layers, the ecosystem. Some lucky agile coaches are asked to lead such a transformational activity, and this book is designed to support them in this quest.

Transformation takes agile coaching beyond working with teams and larger teams to the coaching or consulting, at the enterprise level. In this regard, the coach becomes a trusted advisor whose advice is proactively sought by senior executives seeking to improve their organisation. This consulting role requires a level of maturity regarding the agile mindset and techniques used at the team level and additionally, requires finely honed communication, organisational design and change management skills.

This cookbook has four sections:

- The hors d'oeuvre – starters for the coach and the organisation.
- The entrée – recipes for working with teams.
- Set menus – recipes for programmes and larger teams.
- Transformational dinner parties.

As with a real cookbook containing recipes for food, this book is not intended to be read cover-to-cover in one sitting! Instead, as a chef uses a book of recipes, sections can be read when appropriate to remind a coach of, principles, tools or techniques which they may apply in circumstances when exercising their craft.

Each section starts with an introduction and overview of a topic followed by paragraphs outlining the principal elements and the ingredients of each component.

Many agile coaches start coaching after they have acted as a single team coach, a Scrum Master or a Kanban leader. Consequently, in this guide, I have made little attempt to give guidance regarding the Scrum Ceremonies or the Kanban process, assuming previous mastery of these skills by my reader.

Lastly, it is rare for a transformation to engage just one individual as the agile coach. The initial concept for this book was that it should enable teams of coaches to harmonise their activities and deliver mind-blowing results acting in concert.

I hope that you find this book interesting and engaging! Any feedback will be gratefully received.

The Hors D'oeuvre
Starters for the Coach
and the Organisation

To be a great coach, an individual must obtain some coaching skills and become an agile leader. In the agile world, these skills are broad and outlined in later pages of this book. However, the starting point of being a great coach is to have a profound self-understanding, a detailed knowledge of the basic agile mechanics and then to have a systematic, organised approach to pass these on to agile teams.

In this set of hors d'oeuvre recipes, I look equipping the coach, the agile leader, with some agile principles and techniques to improve their training, mentoring and supporting of teams and organisations.

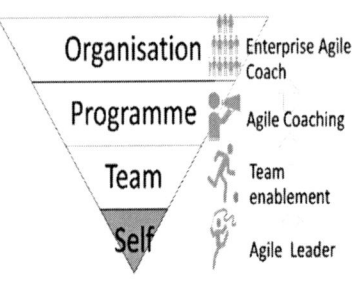

Layers of agile coaching – self

Being an agile leader is not just an individual role; working with others is required. In mature organisations, there are functions such as a Project Management Office (PMO) whose purpose is to facilitate the operational performance and control of teams. When assisting agile teams, however, the PMO often become blockers to new ways of working such that increased performance becomes difficult if not impossible. I have found that a PMO which is a centre of excellence for change has the desire, the relationships, the organisational understanding and some of the skills to become a real catalyst for a transition to agile. Working together with the PMO as an ally often accelerates aspects of agile adoption.

Agile – A Dish with Many Spices

It is said that agile is a dish with many spices, hence the title of this book. Agile is the result of a combination of powerful elements – the spices which make agile successful. There are so many agile flavours that many coaches struggle to provide a simple definition of agile, and I am also not going to try! However, I have distilled these spices into six essential elements – the underlying principles of agile. These elements in my mind are the practical expression of the agile manifesto values and principles.

In my view, a coach should be constantly aware of these six essential elements, in the way the coach interacts with teams and organisations and in the way that they interpret their own agile experiences. An agile coach needs to be especially mindful of each element; when converting a generic agile framework into a specific organisational methodology, and when operating at the enterprise level when rolling out agile across multiple teams.

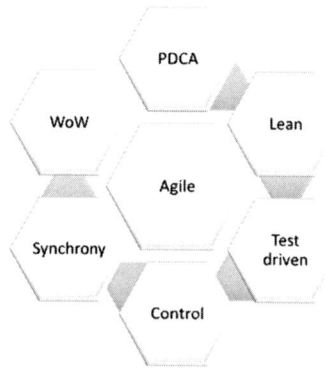

Agile – A dish with many spices
The agile elements

Listing these six essential agile elements here also serves to help the coach to identify cultural or process challenges to an organisation when becoming agile. Clarity also helps the coach to recognise omissions from transformational plans, identify opportunities for improvement or to help diagnose impediments to the transformational process.

PDCA

Plan – Do – Check – Act (PDCA) or the Deming cycle[iii] is the first of these elements and at the centre of the agile, known as "fail fast and learn" or "pivot without fear or remorse". PDCA allows a team, or organisation, to experiment and quickly establish if an idea is going to work out or not.

PDCA can be employed by a coach working with teams during retrospectives or inspect and adapt activities. Alternatively, it can be used less formally, as the coach reacts to situations, adjusting the coaching plan based on observation or feedback from the team.

The PDCA cycle relies upon having the budget to be able to experiment with potential solutions or opportunities and then having the data to verify the outcome. PDCA allows testing or experimentation in limited ways and then to adjust the answer if the original is found not to work as well as anticipated or if it is observed that the results could be bettered. Not all agile activities have an experimental solutioning element, but many teams use PDCA as a means to improve their performance.

PDCA is also a technique which can also be used by an Agile Coach when leading a transformation. For example, in the context of organisational, or process redesign, PDCA can be used to reduce the resistance to change by planning and making organisational or process changes in a pilot mode rather than by making a permanent change at the outset. Using PDCA, the change can be checked and acted upon or adjusted if problems are encountered or if the modification can be further optimised in some way.

However, with PDCA also comes the ability to pivot without mercy should the need arise. This pivot principle is an essential ingredient in the creation of organisational agility and the removal of waste.

Lean Principles

The second element is the use of Lean principles. Some agilists tend to overlook Lean, focussing instead on the mechanics of Scrum, Kanban or SAFe. The mindset embedded in the Lean principles is the combination of beliefs, assumptions and actions with teams. It is the personal, intellectual and leadership foundation for adopting and applying agile principles and practices.

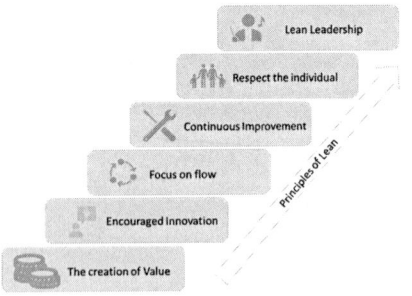

Lean starts with a focus on the creation of Value; that is the worth created for customers, either internal or external.

For example, potential Value is used in selecting initiatives for investment at

Lean principles

the portfolio level. Potential Value is used extensively; prioritising work to be done by a team, measuring achievements and for clarifying requirements.

Keeping a continual focus on the Value delivered is an attribute of excellent agile coaching.

Innovation is at the heart of creative solution delivery, and it is also at the centre of an agile transformation. As identified earlier, it is also here that the PDCA cycles come into play, providing an environment for creativity and encouraged innovation. Agile is used to accelerate Innovation, ensuring that the appropriate solution is offered to customers – quickly. Lean principles are used by an organisation to adapt and relentlessly to improve a solution.

Flow refers to a means of optimising the outputs or Value created by the team. Flow is used to increase the speed of delivery. Using some of the Toyota principles batch sizes of work are restricted and work in progress limits applied. Sometimes in a transformation, the actions to create Flow; small batch sizes and minimising work-in-progress, fly in the face of perceived corporate wisdom. Nevertheless, without the creation of Flow, agile is almost bound not to be effective. Therefore, increasing Flow must be a goal of every agile coach.

Continuous improvement is the sum of the incremental decisions made seemingly small improvements (and mistakes, too!) often have huge effects down the road. Continuous improvement seeks to identify and cut out waste. Waste can occur in product development itself or the delivery process. The team should consider both aspects. The role of the coaching is to continually challenge "how can we make this better, more efficient, more effective". A lean principle is to seek improvement by optimising the whole value stream rather than components of the whole. So sometimes, an agile coach should look at the big picture when seeking optimisation.

Lean principles also identify the human aspects of team working; respect for people and culture. In operating a command-and-control culture, many organisations fail to utilise fully the capabilities of the people they employ. When switching to a more participative culture, the agile coach can often harness this pent-up capability for solution delivery and undertaking the transformational activities.

Lastly, lean leadership is about delegating responsibilities and encouraging continuous improvement. A lean leader communicates the vision, establishes the ecosystem and culture, which allow teams to be efficient and innovate. Often opportunities are missed or take too long if decisions are centralised or made by a single individual. To grow, each individual needs to feel challenged by their work and encouraged to look for better ways of doing things; even if this means altering responsibilities and chains of command.

Being challenged won't be easy at first for those used to being micromanaged because they may feel uncomfortable without being given detailed instructions. Lean leadership is about letting go, developing people, giving teams guardrails, aligning with the corporate goals or intent but empowering those closest to the situation. It is about unlocking the intrinsic capabilities of those involved.

The consequence is that the agile coach not only has to support agile teams; they also need to support the managerial or administrative layers in the organisation at the same time as they too adapt.

As you can see, these lean principles are the foundation of what makes agile different and what makes agile really work. The lean principles provide a continual focus for an agile coach, whether working with a team, with programmes or at the enterprise level.

Test-Driven

The third, often forgotten agile element, relates to quality. Agile QA turns many quality approaches upside down. For example, it resets the waterfall software test V model[iv]; a foundation for many traditional test practices. Agile QA embeds the idea that team defines a requirement to pass a test. In other words, the consideration of quality comes first! With the concept of test definition, first the team is employing a process which enforces a high-quality outcome from the outset rather than using lengthy test cycles at the end of the delivery to establish the desired level of quality.

Acceptance Test-Driven Development (ATDD) and Behaviour Driven Development (BDD) are crucial to agile test-driven, right first time, elements or philosophies. Their use creates essential changes in behaviour which get the team owning the quality of their solution and delivering improvements to their processes.

Test-driven Development (TDD) may also be used by agile coaches to improve the quality of transformational process improvement. TDD can also be used to improve the target operating model by identifying operational scenarios before specifying the design. The coaches facilitate this technique by encouraging those responsible for the redesign to defining the outcomes they desire before redesigning structures or processes. This approach focuses the design activity on the problem to be fixed rather than any pre-conceived ideas of a solution.

Control

Control is the fourth element to be focussed on by agile coaches. A team or organisation cannot be agile if they are not in control. Agile teams broadly use three techniques for control; Scrum, Kanban and a blend of the two called ScrumBan.

Scrum is an empirically controlled way to plan and manage activity. It started with software product development, but now, more often, Scrum is used for any delivery type activity. Scrum provides a series of ceremonies focussed on getting more high-quality work completed quickly. Kanban is a scheduling system with its origin in manufacturing. Kanban helps teams manage the creation of products with an emphasis on continual delivery while not overburdening the team. Kanban helps visualise work and workflow, limiting work in progress so that teams do not start too much work without finishing items. ScrumBan uses the predictive nature of Scrum combined with the management of WIP and Flow from Kanban.

Each of these techniques has an appropriate use. Scrum is most suitable for products and development projects. Kanban is better where the backlog is volatile, for example, with production support. ScrumBan, therefore, sits somewhere in between where it is necessary to combine features of both. For example, with small change or maintenance activities.

Agile project management with Scrum or Kanban is often seen as the only element of an agile methodology. The coach needs to fully understand that these techniques are not the totality of agile, merely the control techniques.

The other aspect of control is that Agile has at its core a self-organising, cross-functional team. Scrum and Kanban teams are both self-organising. Meaning, that there is no overall team leader who decides; which person will do, which task will be worked on first or how a problem will be solved. Instead, these are issues determined by the team collaboratively.

In the team, decisions are made based on observation of outputs rather than on detailed upfront planning, and these actions give agile its new ways of working and its flexibility. This alteration in the ways of working represents a significant shift in managerial mindset for many organisations; the magnitude of which should not be underestimated. Some managers feel incredibly reluctant to let go, and team members often feel exposed as they take on responsibilities for productivity and performance.

Having control in this essential element list seeks to remind each coach of the need for planning and control in the context of the team, the organisation and in the transformation. This cookbook outlines Scrum and Kanban from the dimension of the agile coach. For further reference, I recommend that this book is used in conjunction with the Scrum Guide[v] or the Kanban Maturity Model[vi].

Synchrony

The fifth agile element is synchrony, and it is the essence of agile with larger teams (i.e. more than one Scrum team seven plus or minus two people). Synchrony means that all the iterations start and end at the same time. (Not ideal but at least within a few days of each other.) Synchrony allows continuous integration with its associated means of reducing risk and increasing the quality of the more significantly sized solutions.

When working with larger teams, the agile coach needs to introduce the concepts of synchrony and coordination. These aspects become the primary goals for coaching activities. Successful larger teams synchronise their planning using whole team planning techniques. They also ensure that dependencies are identified, and well-managed. The larger team often has individuals who are responsible for maintaining the continuous integration of completed artefacts or solution components.

Being without synchrony by overlapping iterations adds to the complexity of the activity. As one or more of the teams are always partway through their Sprint cycle; while some are planning a new iteration, others just planned a week ago, and still more teams will plan next week. This situation with planning is replicated with the Sprint Reviews and quality assurance.

Some organisations try to resist efforts to create synchronous delivery cycles proposing overlapping sprint cycles instead. The issue with this approach is that there is never enough time spent on incremental integration (except the end of the initiative). That is that the activity waits to prove the quality of the solution until all the teams are finished as only then can all the components of the solution be integrated and tested as a whole.

Being without synchrony in larger teams makes it very difficult to get an indication of solution quality or to demonstrate a potentially usable solution at the end of each Sprint. This wait-to-the-end approach tactic would mirror a traditional delivery method and not provide the added quality certainty associated with agile. It also reduces the ability to give the entire solution to a customer for feedback or to an operations group for deployment.

Ways of Working

The last agile element to be understood by the agile coach is that the team has control over their ways of working (their WoW). Agile gives teams a relative level of autonomy by ensuring that they are cross-functional and have all the skills needed to complete the solution. Ideally, the team members will be dedicated resources; ensuring that everyone is focused on the same Sprint goal simultaneously without the distraction of a second activity. However, this is dedicated resourcing of initiatives is not always organisationally possible and a coach needs to be pragmatic while preserving the other agile principles in particular that close, even daily, cooperation can happen between the business people and those developing the solution.

Equally important is the level of flexibility within prescribed boundaries. In practice, this means empowering the teams to take the necessary decisions required to deliver their product. It means within specific parameters that the team has the freedom to create ways of working which are valid for them.

The agile coach should encourage teams to think positively about how they can improve. The coach also should ensure that the team collects the metrics to illustrate their performance and substantiate the improvements they have made. This autonomy over ways of working extends into the coaching activity. It is the team which is responsible for all aspects of their activity – not the coach. Meaning that as teams mature, the coach has less influence over the detail of how the work is completed.

As stated earlier, the consideration of each of these six agile elements is essential for the agile coach. Each element provides a different aspect of agile. A competent coach will understand how these elements are blended in different ways, with a different emphasis to give each organisation its unique agile dish. This level of understanding avoids a one-size-fits-all approach and gives agile flexibility as an effective delivery mechanism for nearly all circumstances.

Many agile coaches start on their coaching journeys as Scrum Masters or team members and therefore build and focus their skills activities at the team level. Repetition becomes somewhat inevitable; consequently, organisational performance tends to plateau rather than continuously improving. Keeping these six agile elements in focus ensures that the coaching remains fresh and pertinent to the organisation involved.

Coaching Competency Framework

Another way of considering the coach's skill set is provided by the Agile Coaches Competency framework from the Agile Coaching Institute. The goal of the Agile Coaching Institute is to develop people in the skills and mindsets of great agile coaching. The institute has many resources to get you started as an agile coach, including the Agile Coaching Competency Framework.

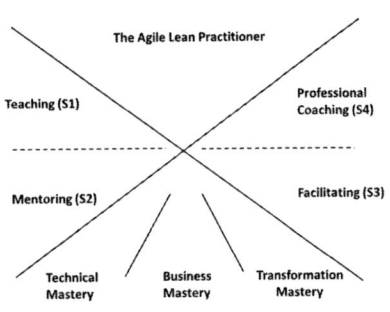

Agile Coaches Competency Framework

This competency framework is a means for coaches to start to think more broadly about their self-development and seeking new ways of interacting with teams and organisations, generally, preventing this plateau effect. The framework has eight segments.

1. Agile Lean Practitioner: The practitioner level skills are the essential understanding which an Agile Coach must-have. It is not about certificates – it is about having practical experience of the application of Lean-Agile techniques in the real-world. It is about the coach's ability to learn from situations. A coach needs an in-depth understanding of the agile frameworks and the Lean principles and most importantly, the ability to communicate theses to team members. This capability is not only at the mechanical level of practices but also at the level of the principles and values which underlie the mechanics.

The four divisions either side of the central horizontal line on the model relate to how a coach interacts or strokes a team. The saying "different strokes for different folks" comes from Situational Leadership. Situational leadership is an approach developed and studied by Kenneth Blanchard and Paul Hersey. It was made famous in The One Minute Manager[vii].

Situational leadership refers to the need for a leader or coach to adjust their style of interaction with a team to suit the developmental needs of that team. The Agile Coaches framework uses a similar four methods of coaching intervention that broadly align to Blanchard.

The approach encourages coaches to take stock of their team, weigh the intervention styles which are possible (the four in the centre of the agile coaching framework) and choose one which best suits the goals and circumstances of their situation.

Situational leadership theory has two concepts: the leadership or coaching process itself, and the developmental level or the maturity of the teams. Situational leadership suggests that the lower the team maturity, the more significant intervention which may be required by the coach. The Agile Coaching Competency model starts with teaching, followed by mentoring, facilitating and finally, professional coaching. These four intervention styles align with the situational leadership model in the following ways.

2. Teaching: This ability aligns to Blanchard's **S1 directing,** and it is the coach's skill to be able to intervene with the appropriate Lean-Agile knowledge, provide this in the right way for the team so that individuals may absorb their new knowledge; enabling them to apply their learning to their situation. Contextual teaching takes the agile practices "out of the book" and directly into the work activity. Broadly from a coaching perspective, this is most often a telling or instructional interaction. The coach is providing specific guidance to the team rather than letting them find their solution. This style of communication is usually one way and is therefore only really appropriate with a newly formed immature team or if the team is in a disaster scenario and immediate results are required.

3. Mentoring: aligns to Blanchard's **S2 coaching** selling or imparting experience. Mentoring is where the coach provides knowledge and guidance to help the team grow or develop specific skills. It involves selling new ideas, explaining techniques and often persuading the team to change. Coaches using this style may create the roles or objectives for others, but they are also open for the team to make suggestions or express opinions. Using this style of intervention, the coach "sells" their ideas for the team to improve performance. A mentoring style intervention is classically used by a coach when the team has learned the basics but needs reminders about some specific aspect of their ways of working.

4. Facilitating: aligns to the Blanchard's **S3 supporting** it is a participative style. Facilitating is where the coach guides the individual's, team's or organisation's process of discovery. The same intervention style can be used at all three levels, S1, S2 and S3, although the actual mechanics of the facilitating would be vastly different. Using the facilitating technique, the coach reminds people of their purpose and definition of success. Then, using a sharing and promoting intervention style where individuals are encouraged to seek their solution to the challenges they face, without content input from the coach. Using this style, a coach may participate by helping people weigh up options as part of a decision-making process, but the ultimate choice of direction is left to the team.

5. Professional Coaching: is Blanchard's **S4 delegating**. Professional coaching is an empowered, hands-off approach. Since the 1980s, the concept of Professional Coaching has evolved and expanded and taken a more generic meaning. Refinement has resulted in several recognised ways of helping people perform more effectively. These include: project, situational and transitional coaching. Project coaching is closely aligned with agile team coaching, which is helping a team achieve a specific result. Situational coaching again mirrors agile coaching but within a context; assisting an individual or a team with a particular challenge to improve performance. Lastly, transitional coaching is about helping the individuals to move from one role to another, a situation frequently encountered in agile transformational activities.

With Professional Coaching, rather than using the coach's expertise or opinion, the team explores and adapts to situations determining their direction. The team has taken responsibility from the coach for its performance. The coach provides minimum guidance within specific guardrails allowing team members to identify then solve problems. However, the coach may be asked by the team from time to time to help them with decision-making or to provide specific inputs.

Three transformational masteries are also included in the Agile Coaching Competency Framework. They relate to working with larger teams and transforming organisations. The three masteries are:

6. Technical Mastery: is the ability of the coach, to use technical expertise, to get pragmatically involved with tooling, technical architecture, designing frameworks for, coding, test engineering or performing some other technical element. The coach's focus is on promoting the agile craft through the organisation's specific ecosystem, by teaching and by providing expertise in agile scaling or structures.

7. Business Mastery: is the ability to apply agile to the business strategy and management frameworks to produce a strategic gain or competitive business advantage. Coaching uses such as Lean Start-Up, product innovation techniques and flow-based process approaches, to deliver these benefits.

8. Transformation Mastery: is partially the subject of this cookbook. It is the ability to facilitate, catalyse and lead rapid organisational change or transformation. This area draws extensively on change management principles, organisation culture, organisation development, systems thinking and other behavioural sciences.

The eight segments of the Agile Coaches Competency framework serve to assist coaches with thinking about their own developmental needs and the application of their understanding and inherent skills.

All the above could tend to lead an inexperienced coach to expect that coaching is very structured and ordered. Unfortunately, this is far from the truth. Research into sports coaching suggests that maximum learning happens not by a structured methodology but near the edge of chaos[viii]. Sports coaching is said to be a dynamic social process founded upon the negotiation between the coach and the athlete. Coaching an agile team in practice is similarly chaotic one the agile basics are understood. As agile concepts are relatively simple to understand but challenging to apply in practice, agile teams need a comparable negotiation element based upon data and reflective analysis.

The following recipes seek to structure and support the coach's introduction, data collection and reflective analysis. However, these tools are not an attempt to identify or espouse best practices. Instead, they provide summaries of agile concepts such that a coach may use these in context to support and develop maturing teams with their negotiated agreement.

Coaching Contract Recipe

For those new to coaching or scrum masters taking the next step, I have started with a recipe which establishes the relationship between a coach and a team. It serves as a reminder that the team is self-managing and therefore coaching is an activity which happens with the permission of the team, not by decree.

Establishing a contract between the Agile Coach and the team is a crucial start point of any competency improvement activity. Having a contract or agreement moderates the potential for coaching chaos; it sets boundaries and ensures clarity for both the team and the coach regarding any interventions, training sessions and feedback. Contracting has more significance with an experienced team compared with a new team which is making its first steps in agile.

Coaching Contract Ingredients

Whether an experienced or new team, the coach needs to remember that it is for the team to identify the nature and content of any coaching they feel that they may require. So while the coach may understand what is necessary, the coach should allow time for the team and its component members of the team to explore what they feel they need. The outcome of good contracting is the agreement of a set of goals for both parties, which they are confident of achieving. Over time, these goals are likely to change; however, this agreement is established before the coaching journey begins.

The coaching contract establishes from the outset the rights, obligations and responsibilities of the coach and the team. For example, it may create an agreement regarding how the team will work on action points in the coach's absence or how often there will be feedback, given in both directions in normal circumstances. It is sure to establish the coach's obligation to maintain confidentiality as well as a non-judgemental approach.

Introducing the Coach to a Team

Sometimes, if you are lucky, the sponsor will present the coach to the team. They can set a coach up for success by being honest – 'I know you are working hard. Nonetheless, due to our inexperience, we are encountering challenges as we implement our new ways of working. Given that this is new for all of us, I've brought in an experienced Agile Coach to support you.'

On the other hand, kicking off a coaching a new team may be part of a transformation, and personal introductions are not made. Sometimes, a coach will arrive and find that the team has not had any expectation set. Sometimes, someone else may have been coaching, and for various reasons, there may be no handover at all! In this instance, the coach will need to set up a coaching contract with the team.

Sometimes, a coach will need to explain what an agile coach can do – describing how the coach can support the team. These situations will start the dialogue between the coach and the team. However, due to experience, it is often a conversation which, is usually guided by the coach.

At the outset, the coach needs to understand the coach's operating triangle. The triangle provides the context in which the coach is to act.

Before starting to coach a team, the coach needs to understand the organisational context; that is what is the organisation going to achieve by the output of the team. If the organisation is adopting agile, the coach must understand why this is and coach the teams to fulfil these objectives. Exploring the critical success factors is an excellent way for a coach to understand the organisational context.

In mature agile shops, the coach needs to understand the relationship between sponsor, coach and team. Based upon analysis of this situation, the Agile Coach can decide upon the nature and content of the potential interventions and the likely kind of the support required.

The coach also needs to understand the sponsor's expectations of the team and the coach for that matter! A good coach seeks to ensure that alignment exists between the team and the sponsor.

Sometimes, the team's past projects may have built a poor relationship with the sponsor due to poorly managed expectations or missed deliveries in the past. This history can have a bearing on the team as they adopt new ways of working and can be an adverse influence on the openness and honesty valued by agile.

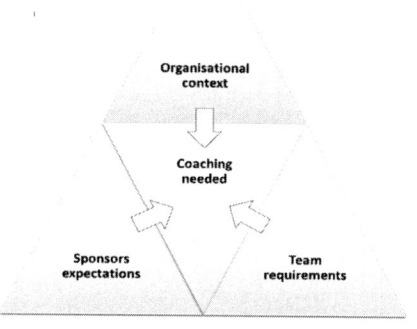

The coach's operating triangle

Sometimes this is tricky, as the coach may discover that they also need to influence or coach the sponsor, to achieve a successful outcome. The required support from the coach is, therefore, a balance of three factors; the organisational context, the requirements of the team and the skills of the coach.

Lastly, coaching should be provided in the context of the team's requirements. It is natural for a new or inexperienced team to look to the Agile Coach to provide a degree of structure. Having a coaching plan with a sequence of activities in your mind or written down will help.

The Coach's Plan Recipe

Many times, after a game or event, a sports coach indicates that their team needs to improve a particular aspect of their performance. The sports coach develops a coaching plan as a result of the game just finished. The same is true of agile teams. An agile coach does the same, analyses team performance and decides what they need to do to help the team improve. The result is an agile coach's plan.

Just as with sports teams, developing a coaching strategy for an agile team also takes time to prepare. A good coach's plan gives structure and de-risks the delivery during the transition to agile. The plan helps to inform the team, the leaders of team members and sometimes senior management of potential developmental needs or the changes needed. It provides everyone with an awareness of the journey so that they may enable and support team members through the process.

An agile transformation is a significant endeavour and typically is undertaken while operational activities continue. It is, therefore, essential that the coach's plan minimises the risk to current business operations and reduces operational disruption.

Coach's Plan Ingredients

Following a coach's plan gives structure to the coaching activities. It starts from a generic "first meeting" situation and builds through kick-off and development. Modified on a regular basis; the plan identifies the need for coaching and training over time. Initially, this plan will be generic. However, with each iteration, the coach's plan will become unique to the needs of a specific team. Over time, the coach's plan will increasingly be based upon the health check analysis referred to previously.

To be able to operate successfully, a coach needs to establish a strong, trusting relationship with the team. So, it is essential to think about engagement at the outset. You will need to outline your credentials to be a coach and the

Reviewing the coaching plan

value that you can bring to your team. From experience, I would suggest for the first meeting at "let's get to learn something about each other" level rather than diving into agile theory or techniques.

When a coach meets a team for the first time, sometimes there is a temptation to launch into your past, describing who you are and what you want to achieve with the team. Forgetting that it is their team, and the question is more about what they want to accomplish with your help. When getting to know a new team, the perfect starting point could be the question. "How will the outputs of this activity fit into…" Allowing a team to explain their understanding of the vision, their perception of work ahead and their anticipation of the challenges they expect. May set the scene and give a good indicator of team maturity or capability. However, a first introduction, no matter how introduced is not a time to solve the initial problems, but rather to express your curiosity and learn more.

Activity	Objectives	Date
INITIAL Team CONTACT – Communication opportunity #!	Present a clear message indicating to the team, their leaders and or managers that you will be guiding them through the upcoming changes to adopt agile working. (Coaches note: The messaging should be transparent and clear to avoid speculation and rumour. In communication, you will also need to address any fears or doubts regarding the future. It should also outline what teams can expect from an Agile Coach – clarification regarding roles and responsibilities. This meeting is intended as an initial notification that there will be more to come in terms of conversations, meetings, training, coaching and support.)	

The best coaching outcome for this initial meeting is to leave the team ready for what might come next. So, as you reveal elements of your coaching plan to the team, you will increase their understanding of the way you operate and the purpose for your next and subsequent meetings. You may also suggest the team might think about things they wish to change, to learn more about or to remove obstacles to progress which they have identified.

Activity	Objectives	Date
	(Coaches notes: The first meeting with the transformation team is essential because it sets the scene and establishes the relationship between the coach and the team. It should re-enforce and build upon any prior communications the team has received, including the organisational context and rationale for adopting Agile.	
First meeting with the team	1. Introduce: Detail the change in working practices and how these may affect the traditional recipients' roles. 2. Explain: Showcase your (the agile change leader's or coaches) position and outline how the changes are to be adopted or implemented. Be candid about the impacts and effects will have on team members, managers and team leaders. The objective is to establish an initial alignment to the journey ahead. 3. Support: Detail the plans for support, coaching and formal training throughout the process. Explain the changes to facilitating functions such as PMO and Finance. a. Supply information regarding the training plans. Discuss steps in the implementation and the critical elements of the timeline as it pertains to the team and stakeholder expectations. b. Provide a summary of the planned coaching sessions, the agenda or schedule for the coaching – this gives clarity regarding how you will support the team. It also explains to	

		managers and senior leaders how you plan to coach their staff through the activities.	
		c. You may also introduce plans for trials of prototypes and change (the PDCA cycles) if applicable.	
		4. Discuss: Providing time for those affected to engage with the concepts of agile, express their fears and perceptions of agile.	

Use of a Team Health Check Model

Many organisations wish to establish ways of measuring and visualising how their teams are doing. These organisations often use the term "maturity model", and they typically involve some progression through predefined different levels. These models often infer that the team systematically progresses through several pre-defined states. Yet, this is far from the reality most teams readily advance in certain aspects of agile but leave other important issues lagging in their application. One of the classic lagging aspects in my experience is often the one of quality assurance – the teams focus on Scrum or Kanban and forget solution quality!

The initial intent of these types of maturity models is usually relatively innocent. In larger organisations, coaches or managers want to get an idea regarding where they should seek improvement efforts, identify systemic problems or help teams become more self-aware so they can focus their continuous improvement. However, all too often these models may become a means for the organisation to "judge" teams.

I prefer to use the term health check model because the use of the word maturity doesn't reflect my intent and purpose. Rather than the team progressing through different levels, the health check model allows the agile coach and the team to reflect upon team health at a single point in time. The model is helpful as the team dynamics could be changed by new people joining or the team may have encountered a challenging situation, or there may have been a change in the agile coach. The health check model serves as a record of team development at a point in time.

Looking at several team health checks over time allows the team and the coach to jointly identify areas for additional training, coaching or establish the need for systemic, external to the team, organisational improvements. Without some analysis, the improvement work by the coach is very much subjective (how will the coach decide what needs to be improved, and how will you know if things are moving in the right direction). A systemic PDCA approach using a health check model with clear visualisation can reduce some of the guesswork and introduces objectivity.

The health check, coupled with a coaching plan provides minimal documentation which can facilitate a change in the individual providing the agile coaching should this become necessary. The health check and coaching plan also offer a record of the status of the coaching should an unexpected absence of a coach occur.

Team Health Check Recipe

Coaches often ask how often they should check the health of a team? In stable market environments, perhaps monthly is too frequent, yet half-yearly seems too seldom. Quarterly feels about right for team input to the health assessment or when coaches are changed, or the team has a significant change in membership. During new team start-up or evolution, then more frequently rather than less frequently would seem appropriate. Of course, the coaches may refer to the health check analysis more often as they provide coaching to the team and observe the outcomes.

The Health Check Ingredients

- Be clear candid about your motives for introducing the health check model. It is about team performance improvement and your ability to help the team. It's not about judgement.
- Decide when and how to gather the information needed. I suggest primarily through one-to-one communication, as people can be more open and support this with a collective team session. The data collected should be anonymised, and the process should attempt to be engaging and fun.
- Involve the teams in how the model is applied and let them modify it as they see fit.

- Team acceptance matters more than the consistency of the data. If team A chooses a slightly modifies the set of questions because they have been together longer than team B, that's fine!
- Make sure that there is not an incentive to "game" the health check model. There should be no secondary reason for a team to want to look good. The health check is purely about the identification of the support they need from their coach.
- Visualise the data. The more evident and intuitive the visualisation is, the more likely it is to be considered and used. Having a visual representation will encourage the team to be able to see how they are improving over time.
- Beware of comparing teams. If team A is mostly plain sailing and team B is mostly encountering challenges, that doesn't mean that team A is better than B. It could just say that team A has a more straightforward context or a more optimistic outlook, or that team B is being more honest about their struggles. Either way, the use of the health check is to identify the need for support, and from this information, it looks as though team B may need some!
- The coach should not just present the data but should also offer the follow up in the form of a proposed coaching plan. After all, the team itself is responsible for its performance. Such questions like; is this model helping you? "If we stopped doing these health checks, would you miss them?", "How could we make this model and coaching plan more useful to you?". The model itself and of course, your coaching way of applying it, also needs to improve continuously.

Agile Health Check Template

Team		Coach	
		Sprint or iteration #	
Date of observation			
Agile roles and responsibilities			
Strengths		Challenges	
Tailoring the agile process			
Strengths		Challenges	
Requirements analysis			
Strengths		Challenges	
Backlog management			
Strengths		Challenges	
Estimation			
Strengths		Challenges	
Agile risk management			
Strengths		Challenges	
Release planning			
Strengths		Challenges	
Test planning			
Strengths		Challenges	
Control and management of the schedule			
Strengths		Challenges	
Continuous improvement			
Strengths		Challenges	
Long-lived teams			
Strengths		Challenges	

Scaling Scrum	
Strengths	Challenges
Governance compliance	
Strengths	Challenges
Change control	
Strengths	Challenges

The Questions for Team Development

Self-managing teams may have a resistance to coaching "inflicted" on them by a coach. They may wish to guide their progress themselves. As an alternative to a health check, I have used the GROW approach (standing for Goal, Reality, Options and what Will they change). The GROW questions can be used by a coach in facilitation or professional coaching mode to assist teams with the creation of their development plan.

The GROW model[ix] is a series of four questions which a coach may use in a conversation about team or individual development. Grow stands for Goal, Reality, Options, Will. In this, the team or individual defines what they wish to improve, they place that desire in the context of their reality, evaluate options and then decide what they will do to achieve their stated goal.

Goal	Possible questions:
("What do you want?" or "What is the team trying to achieve?")	What do you want to achieve?
	How do you wish to operate?
	What are the objectives of your initiative?
	What roles and responsibilities have you defined?
	Are your current ways of working clear?
	What aspects of your team do you need, or want, to develop?

Reality (What is happening now)	Possible questions: How much of your time do you currently spend on? How do you know XX is not working?
Options (What could you do)	Possible questions: How would this be if you changed XX?
Will (What will you do / Way forward)	Possible questions: To move things forward, what is the first step you need to take? When are you going to do it? What support do you think you need or want from me your coach? On a scale of 1 – 10, how committed are you to taking that action?

The Questions for Team Development Ingredients

These questions could be used during a facilitated retrospective or an inspect and adapt event, to encourage the team to think about continuous improvement. GROW could also have relevance during professional coaching activities, especially in transitional coaching. Coaches should be aware that the power of the technique would probably diminish with overuse.

An alternative to GROW is to use a decision balance sheet. This technique allows a team to weigh up options by identifying the pros and cons of a particular course of action. It's a simple linear chart completed as per this example.

Alternatives	Pros	Cons

A decision balance sheet could be used during a retrospective or indeed at any other time when a team or an individual wishes to evaluate options.

As there is a variety of techniques which can be used to identify coaching needs, I have found it useful to maintain a coaches diary. The diary is particularly helpful when I am coaching more than one team as it reminds me of the current team situation. Should I be sick or unavailable, the coaching diary also allows another coach to pick up where I left off.

Coaching Diary Recipe

A coaching diary or log is a simple way for you to debrief after every interaction with a team. It not only helps you understand the situation of your team, but it also helps the coach to understand herself as well. The coaching diary can also provide relevant input to the coach's reflective practice.

The coaching diary allows the coach to reflect on team maturity and plan coaching sessions and record the impacts of each. The attendance record enables the coach to identify the coverage of the intervention and allows the identification of a team member who may have missed the training or coaching activity.

I am not suggesting that the agile coach would record their observations and interactions in every scrum, although some may find this useful. I am suggesting that the diary records significant coaching activities and the associated results. It is to mark the nature of the intervention, the style used, the desired outcome or competency improved.

Coach's Diary Template

Agile Coach's Diary

Team	Team Member
Date	

Coaching session attendance

Team member	Role	1	2	3	4	5	6	7	8	9	10

Coaching Session	# 1	Date:	
		Desired Outcome	
	Remarks		

Coaching Session	# 2	Date:	
		Desired Outcome	
	Remarks		

Add further sections as needed

The Reflective Practice Recipe

Reflective practice is a kind of coach's retrospective. In its basic form, it is about it is thinking about a coaching intervention, the outcome and what to improve for next time.

Reflective Practice is the ability to analyse to continue to learn and enhance coaching skills. The coaching plan and coaching diary provide inputs to the coach's reflection. The reflection could be a shared activity, working with other coaches, or it could be self-analysis. There is much more to Reflective Practice than is contained here. It is worth a coach taking the time to look into this subject in greater detail.

The principle is a practical example of double-loop learning[x], as suggested by Chris Argyris; the technique allows the coach to scrutinise the theory with the application. What outcome was expected compared to the actual result? The purpose of Reflective Practice is to change or improve underlying assumptions, values and behaviours of the coach. Its use enables the coach to deal with real and complex situations exploring and adapting their style and type of intervention as situations occur.

Reflective Practice Ingredients

Reflective Practice is an opportunity for a coach to learn and improve their coaching skills.

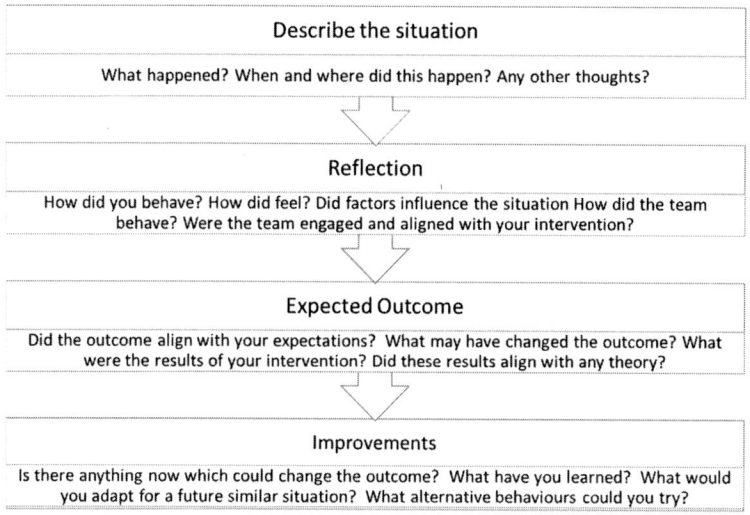

The four steps of Reflective Practice

Sometimes it is challenging to take a timeout to think about the coaching interventions. A prerequisite, like a team retrospective, is to set aside a little time for review and reflection. Reflective Practice is a four-step process; some say that it a cycle.

The first step is to decide on a situation from which the coach wishes to learn. Perhaps an intervention didn't go as well as intended or maybe where team feedback indicates the need for a better coaching approach.

The key to the second step is reflection; where the coach needs to develop the skill of objectively reflecting on the experience. Sometimes being honest with oneself is difficult, and this is where reflective practice as a shared activity could be beneficial.

The third step is to evaluate the difference between the expected outcome of the intervention and the actual result. Sometimes metrics will have a part to play. In other circumstances, the comparison may only be behavioural.

The final step is to decide what needs to improve and to develop a plan for how the coaching intervention should change in the future. This step may involve the coach doing some further learning, revisiting the coaching plan for a team or preparing additional notes for future use.

So far, I have talked about how a coach may organise and improve themselves. However, coaching may happen from line management and functions like the PMO. The next few recipes speak about why and how to change the PMO.

Changing the PMO Recipe

Most large organisations typically have lots of initiatives in-flight at any one time and may have additional activities under consideration for investment or undergoing some form of prioritisation. Consequently, many organisations have a function to manage this situation known as a Project Management Office or PMO. The PMO is commonly a function which provides a level of oversight of upcoming and in-flight activities, and in doing so, it defines and maintains the organisational standards for solution delivery.

None of these PMO actions is particularly independent; they rely on the collaboration and conformity of the delivery teams. Over time, the PMO has probably standardised and introduced toolsets, techniques and processes which have become intrinsic to the organisational DNA and its traditional project delivery ecosystem. The result is that the PMO places demands on teams so that they can perform their function of organising, overseeing and managing the risks. The consequence of these demands is that they may block or stall agile adoption if the agile coach does not counter these requirements. If the PMO has processes based upon waterfall delivery when teams switch to agile, I have found that conflict and confusion results. In this situation, the agile coach, therefore, not only has to coach the transitioning team; often, the PMO also requires support. Assisting the PMO to redesign its function, so teams are encouraged on their agile journey is a critical part of the coach's remit in my view!

Often, when the PMO hears that an agile coach is working with teams, the PMO function often asks the simple question: "what is the role of the Project

Management Office in an agile organisation?". They are often shocked to hear that as custodians of the project delivery methods that they have a fundamental and essential role to play in agile transformation.

Although the PMO's responsibilities inevitably shrink in terms of operational control, being replaced by the empowered and self-organising agile teams. The PMO role expands into organising portfolio-planning events, big room planning sessions and large scale inspect and adapt activities. This change in PMO emphasis requires explanation and often coaching to be understood.

The effort of working with a PMO often has significant benefits for an agile coach. Often the PMO is the source of training, coaching, documentation, guidance and metrics on the organisation's best practice of project management and execution these resources provide organisational context for the coach. The PMO is usually exceptionally well-placed to act as a catalyst and enabler of the agile change. This is due to its extensive knowledge base of the organisation, the in-flight and the upcoming initiatives. Once the agile adoption has moved into the normalisation stage, then the PMO is the logical organisational home for Agile Coaches.

However, in some organisations, the PMO may also be merely administrative function; taking minutes, booking rooms and the like. There are almost as many different PMOs as there are organisations! Yet even in an administrative style PMO, there will be some degree of ownership or authority over the solution delivery ecosystem.

The PMO is a prime example of an organisational construct which may block or slow down the speed of agile adoption. I have found that the slowing down of agile adoption is especially true when the PMO's function is to manage or minimise risks associated with solution delivery. The Agile, self-managing team paradigm challenges many of how organisations have traditionally delivered change. In some instances, this self-managing aspect challenges the modus operandi of many PMOs. It is therefore essential to adapt the PMO processes and to change their expectations before an agile team encounters PMO resistance themselves.

Changing the PMO Ingredients

Redesigning a PMO is relatively simple and a great use of value stream mapping techniques. In one transformation, I tried to do this mapping myself. Mistake! I have since learned that the most effective way of getting a PMO to change is for them to reform themselves! Creating and critiquing the delivery value stream is one way of helping the PMO to adapt to agile.

Getting the PMO to change often exposes individual concerns about capabilities and knowledge. The individuals in the PMO understand what the PMO does but may not have insight regarding why. PMO rules and rituals often build up over time as a result of guidance or managerial decisions. Very often, there is a difference between what is written and taught regarding the PMO processes and techniques used and the actual operation.

I have found that mapping the PMO processes; then using Aristotle's five Ws; Who, What, When, Where, Why works but my analysis has been often challenged by PMO leads. I now hold a collaborative value-stream mapping session with the PMO and repeat this revising their processes as the transformation progresses.

Before the value stream mapping session, I will often need to do some agile values and principles training with the PMO team. I then use the PMO to define its "as-is model" and document their process and templates. Then I move on to establishing the to-be model, that is how the PMO will operate once a significant part of the portfolio has adopted agile. In this to-be model, revised processes and templates will feature. This remodelling of the PMO allows the agile team training to include governance, delivery standards and other relevant process changes.

A PMO can never act in isolation, so changes in PMO processes impact others. The changes need communications to be prepared so that all concerned (stakeholders) understand what is changing and why. I have found that it is essential to get the PMO community to provide this communication rather than the agile coaches.

The Lean-Agile PMO Recipe

As an agile adoption progresses, the PMO becomes increasingly impacted, and a radical reinvention of the PMO is often required. If only one or two teams are using agile, then the impact on the PMO can be minimalised. However, as adoption gathers momentum, the foundations of the organisational delivery ecosystem increasingly need to be changed. Which inevitably means that the PMO will need to completely revise its delivery standards so that teams can use agile within the context of the organisational governance framework. At this point, an agile coach needs a strong relationship with the PMO, so they can appropriately influence the ecosystem redesign.

In organisations where agile is maturing, each team will define and continuously refine their delivery process. In these circumstances, the PMO needs to take a proactive view of how teams are developing and accept that at the micro-level teams may optimise their delivery methods while conforming to accepted organisational practices at the macro-level.

The consequence is that the PMO needs to redefine itself, bringing in new working practices, training and toolsets to support the new ways of working. When redefining the PMO, the coach needs to consider the fact that it is unlikely that all activities will convert to Agile simultaneously, so often the redesign needs to give the PMO the ability to manage both Agile and traditional activities.

I have called this redesigned function the Lean-Agile PMO so to avoid confusion between the new ways of working and a traditional PMO. Why lean? The lean objective is to design a PMO which delivers maximum value to its customers (stakeholders) with as little wasted effort as possible. The redesign also facilitates activities to minimise waste and provides mechanisms for relentless continuous improvement. Why agile? The agile objective is to provide an ecosystem and collaborative working practices such that activities are demonstrably delivered as fast as possible, irrespective of delivery methodology, with "just enough" governance and oversight so that risks are well-managed, and success is assured.

Implementing the Lean-Agile PMO Ingredients

Implementing a new Lean-Agile PMO function may be a new challenge to some agile coaches, and many will be able to facilitate others to do the redesign for them. I have used an eight-stage process which involves defining the functions of the Lean-Agile PMO.

The process starts with the PMO functions – what functions do the stakeholders feel the PMO should provide? A means of doing this is to seek clarification regarding the benefits which the organisation wishes to see from the redefined PMO.

Reinventing the PMO

The second step is Research. In some instances, the agile coach and the PMO leadership may need to research how the Lean-Agile PMO should support the new agile ways for working. Often, research is necessary regarding how processes should be modified or replaced to best achieve the organisational goals.

Using a multi-disciplined team to plan, design and build the new Lean-Agile PMO service makes sense as it replicates the agile ways of working. I have seen some PMO teams use Scrum to control this process development and implementation. They start with preparing a roadmap and then build out sections of the service in increments. It is critical at this redesign stage not to forget that no PMO operates in isolation. Therefore, during implementation, a thorough communications plan needs to be put in place and used.

As the PMO usually owns the Product, Programme and Project delivery methodologies, the PMO needs to consider how the organisation will adopt the new agile ways of working. What constraints, if any the organisation will place on the agile teams. The coaches alongside the PMO need to decide the agile implementation strategy.

Iteration is a means of implementing solutions quickly, to learn from the experience and then adjust. Repetition is a way of using the PDCA Deming cycle to gradually refine and improve the partnership between the Lean-Agile PMO and the solution delivery teams.

As the organisation considers new ways of working, the question of suitable tooling arises. Many tools used for traditional delivery use the wrong operational premise for agile delivery. New tooling is therefore often required to facilitate the solution delivery teams and the PMO itself.

The test and learn stage takes into account many different dimensions. It is the check act of the Deming cycle. It checks the new team construct, the solution delivery process, the use of the agile framework, the latest techniques and the tooling and acts (adjusts) according to the findings. It is during this stage that feedback from those outside the PMO, in the teams and among the stakeholders becomes essential. This is when the listening elements of the communications plan are used exhaustively.

Lastly, the Lean-Agile PMO needs to consider its metrics – how does the PMO know that it is meeting or exceeding the expectations of its stakeholders and providing the benefits which they identified that they required in the first step.

Serving Suggestions the Hors D'oeurves

These hors d'oeuvre recipes establish the essential elements of agile and giving the coach tools to measure progress. A great coach offers support and assistance to those he or she is coaching to help them implement change and achieve desired goals. A great coach has a refined sense of curiosity, coupled with a hunger for learning. According to Imornefe Bowes and Robyn L. Jones in their paper "Working on the Edge of Chaos[xi]", real learning only happens when a team's or individual's perception is changed. They go on to say this is not by the understanding of agile but by working with a coach practically seeking and identifying new patterns and results. I have attempted to point towards tools used in sport, as similar situation points, to means to improve performance and achievement of goals. (The coaching diary and the team health check are starters in this direction. In the next section, containing entrée recipes, I introduce the coach's plan.)

The coach must be relevant and credible when discussing today's issues and technology. It is essential that a coach does not become complacent in this regard. A successful agile coach cannot stay in the past. In my experience, as soon as you are comfortable with your growth in a particular area, that is the minute when your development stops, and your relevance as the coach starts to reduce.

Professional development is often a team effort. In agile coaching terms, this means that it is not solely up to you – the team can often help themselves, particularly as they gain in maturity. A great coach is someone that can deliver performance improvement without creating resentment.

Lastly, in these hors d'oeuvre recipes, I have looked at changing the PMO. According to the PMI, over seventy per cent of organisations have a PMO[xii]. It is consequently not unreasonable for an agile coach to expect to PMO and PMO function in its many guises. I have therefore included some recipes for changing the PMO in preparation for introducing agile to teams.

The Entrée – Recipes for Working with Teams

Having introduced the hors d'oeuvre, we now move on to the agile entrée; the main course – working with teams. Small teams regularly delivering are the critical tenet of an agile organisation. I identified this role as team enablement as the coach is an experienced Scrum Master, Kanban Flow Manager or someone called an agile coach. Typically, the Scrum Master or Kanban Flow Manager is internal to the team. While the agile coach, like a sports coach, does not usually have coaching duties in addition to playing. In some circumstances, the Scrum Master may also be responsible for one or up to three teams, and in this sense may also be an external party.

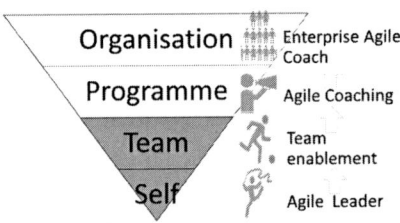

Coaching layers – team enablement

Having worked with many teams, I've come to trust a few tools that I have found to deliver value. For example, retrospective formats or risk management approaches. However, what works for one team doesn't necessarily work for the next. So, in this section, I have outlined some of the recipes that I have used and collected overtime for working with teams.

Diagnose	Adapt	Communicate	Advance
Diagnose the issue	Adapt coaching	Use of the appropriate intervention style	Enable the team by illustrating the measurable improvements
Establish the team or individuals desire to improve	Depending upon team maturity and desire to change	Working with the team	
Establish measures for improvement			Facilitate the next steps

Situational based coaching

No doubt, as a coach, you will be working with teams using different frameworks. The recipes used in this section are not agile framework-specific but generic meals which can be consumed in many different circumstances. Don't be afraid to fight the framework! Learn the essential differences, and you will find more commonality across the frameworks than you may at first suppose.

Not all teams will react in the same way to a similar coaching method, (refer again to the section on coaching styles in the Coaching Competency section). The form of the coaching intervention in Situational Leadership is based upon a four-stage model; initially diagnosing the team maturity and willingness to change. The second stage is for the coach to prepare a coaching plan; adapting their coaching approach to match the situation of the team.

In communicating, the coach is interacting with the team in order to improve. The final stage is to measure the results so to enable or motivate the team by clearly illustrating their success. Advancing the team is where the coaching diary recipe comes into use. Just as a sporting coach may use the metric of time when working with a long-distance runner. So, the agile coach uses focussed metrics to establish the current baseline, then advance team performance.

Team Charter – Recipe

At some point, your team will wish to establish the rules by which it wants to operate. I use a lightweight document as a team charter which serves as a reference point for team decisions. The charter can be referenced during team retrospectives and serves as a record for functions external to the team; such as during an internal audit.

The initial meeting is probably too early for this activity unless the agile adoption has reached a certain level of maturity already in the organisation. A typical team charter may include:

- The behaviours and ways of working to which all members of the team aspire.
- A decision to use Kanban or Scrum or a combination of both techniques.
- How the team plans meetings will be conducted, the frequency, or to how to accommodate individuals' working preferences or nonworking commitments.
- Roles and responsibilities – this is of specific importance for distributed teams.
- Agreement what they will do when any new members join.
- In the case of offshore teams, the charter should outline the team's "golden hours" and means of communication.
- The key metrics which the team may use to control their activities.

It may be that the definition of the team charter could naturally fit into the agile process tailoring activity for most teams. The language in the charter has to be clear to everyone. In the case of geographically dispersed teams, where people may have a different native language, the text used in the charter must be simple to avoid ambiguity in interpretation.

Rapid Team Start-Up Recipe

The rapid team start-up model can be used when the agile methods have been pre-defined, and when there has been a call to action for a new team. You could also use the model with an experienced team when agile methods are still being defined. However, if the agile working practices are still being defined, then you would expect the team to spend longer in the agile process tailoring activity.

Activity	Objectives
Training	Provide training to the team on the methodology, introduce the roles, the agile mindset and the new quality assurance approach. For an experienced team, this may be a reminder or summary training activity, or it could be something more meaningful in terms of capability development.
Agile Process tailoring workshop	Run a process-tailoring workshop, walk the team through the essential aspects of the agile delivery process. Agree on the team charter. Decide on the ways of team working, the documentation they will need to produce and how the delivery process will operate. Select the lifecycle, the release and test strategy. Walking through the agile process goals one at a time and addressing the decision points of each one and discussing roles and responsibilities.
Getting Started	Getting started involves identifying the things the team knows and then establishing what they need to know. These work items form the backlog for the initial Sprint or Inception Stage. If you like, it is the backlog to create the backlog.
Prepare an initial plan	This plan is usually a plan to get to a plan. The plan for the initial stages may have more tasks in it than requirements. The initial schedule of activities should identify when they will make a commitment to the release plan and sprint goals to their stakeholders.

Roles and Responsibilities Recipes

The three scrum roles describe the critical duties of those individuals in the scrum team. They aren't by necessity job titles but Scrum roles performed by the team. Meaning that any job title, even existing ones, can perform one or more of the functions. The consequence is that roles and responsibilities need to be defined and agreed for each team and recorded in a way that the team can refer to if needed.

As the essence of Scrum is empirical, self-organisation and continuous improvement, the three roles give a minimum definition of responsibilities and accountability to allow teams to deliver the solution effectively. However, it is a minimum. Many teams require further roles and specialisms to complete their solution.

It is a principle in Scrum, that team members should have generic skill sets, yet for many teams in many organisations, this is not always possible. I have found that minimally documenting the agreed roles and responsibility is of great help, especially with distributed teams or teams where the membership has more than one paternal language.

In Kanban, there are no predefined roles. However, two terms have come into common usage. The Service Delivery Manager is a role description similar to the Scrum Master in that they are concerned with improving the efficiency of the delivery workflow. The second role is the Service Request Manager, who acts in the same way as a Scrum Product Owner in that they reflect the needs and expectations of the customer to the team. The Service Request Manager is a role typically fulfilled by middle management who will have in-depth knowledge organisation's value stream.

The agile coach should ensure that they facilitate the roles and responsibilities conversation such that all team members receive clarity. This clarity has added importance with teams with a remote or offshore membership.

Agile Process Tailoring Recipe

In an agile process-tailoring workshop, a coach or the Scrum Master walks the team through the essential aspects of the agile delivery process and the team discusses then decides how they're going to work together. Typically, the initial conversation will be the discussion clarifying what they are to achieve, but it will swiftly move on to discussions about ways of working, roles and responsibilities, the delivery process and the level of documentation and so on. Particularly with the new team, the coach needs to allow time for these discussions, as they are an inherent part of the stages in the Form, Storm, Norm, Perform stages of the Tuckman model[xiii].

With some teams, a fundamental discussion will inevitably occur regarding the use of Scrum or Kanban as the primary means of control. I have found the creation of the team's delivery value chain diagram very helpful in documenting the outputs of this workshop.

Agile Process Tailoring Ingredients

During team start-up or Inception, I establish three approximately 90-minute sessions for agile process tailoring with the hope that I will not require all this time. If I anticipate some training needed, then the first session may be longer to allow for the instruction.

The time needed for agile process tailoring is typically driven by the team's agile maturity. Smaller, more experienced crews will very likely get this done quickly but the larger the team, or more extensive the range of experience, the longer it will take.

If the team is new to agile, then this process tailoring activity could well be part of rapid team start-up activities as proposed earlier.

With a new team, the during agile process tailoring the coach is likely to be operating in a teaching or mentoring mode. With more experienced teams, the coaching mode is more one of facilitation.

Process tailoring is also an essential element with large teams. Larger teams divided into smaller feature or component teams, using frameworks such as SAFe or LeSS, harmonised agile process tailoring is critical. From a coaching point of view, process tailoring should occur while working with the complete larger team rather than with the individual smaller teams.

Teams planning to use Kanban would define the Kanban rules and classes of service during agile process tailoring.

Definitions of Ready and Done Ingredients

There are reasons why you want to encourage your team to tailor their process, not least of which is continuous improvement.

1. Every team is unique and faces a specific situation created by the solution they are to develop. It is a foundational principle of agile that each team should own their process, so they can work together effectively.

2. In the retrospective, the team seeks to improve its delivery process. Often a commonly prescribed process doesn't quite fit all situations. In the retrospective, the team aims to adapt the processes they previously agree on process tailoring seeking to become more efficient as they do so.

3. The team needs a shared vision as to how to work together the conversation tailoring the process establishes this common understanding. For teams to work together effectively, they need to agree on how they're going to do so. Without a shared vision, a team will often flounder.

4. Teams attempt to optimise and identify their chosen ways of working to make themselves as efficient as possible. In these agreements, they will establish the means to reduce work in progress (WIP) to work at a sustainable pace and to eliminate waste wherever they can.

5. There is nearly always a need to document the solution in development. The creation of documentation aspects needs to be part of the agile delivery process. The teams need to adopt agile documentation strategies which allow the production of documentation as lightweight and yet sufficiently detailed to meet the "just enough" requirements.

6. Generally during the agile process tailoring, the team also agrees to a Definition of Ready. The Definition of Ready is a working agreement between the team and the product owner on what readiness means. It is essential as being ready enables the team to plan when a work item can be completed. Having the status of ready is a means for the product owner to indicate to the team that a work item in the backlog is ready for development. It is typically a product owner responsibility to ensure that the definition of ready is established.

7. A Definition of Done should also be agreed by each team, or potentially across teams if they are working on a single product release and sets the standard that all requirements should meet before work items can be said to be completed or finished. The definition of done helps ensure that the product owner and the development team are clear when a work item is complete or not.

Requirements Analysis Recipe

With traditional projects, stakeholders are conditioned that they must get all their requirements established early in the activity life-cycle. Consequently, they desperately try to define as many potential requirements as they can. These requirements may include things think they might need, but they aren't totally sure about that at the time. They know if they don't get the needs established, then it will be hard to get them added later. This is because of the change management process, which had been put in place in waterfall activities to make modifications very difficult once the requirements are baselined.

With agile delivery, the process of defining requirements is different and often needs an explanation for stakeholders. However, from a coaching perspective, there needs to be some definition of the scope and purpose of an activity, or it is bound to fail.

Requirements Analysis Ingredients

Experience shows that it is better to establish the whole scope at high-level at first, for the team to get a feel for the entire breadth of the solution required. Rather than to focus narrowly on the detail of one small aspect. However, sometimes the full scope of an endeavour is unknown or unclear. In this instance, the exploration of breadth will have gaps; known unknowns, and unknown unknowns.

To be clear, this breadth of scope statements do not limit the activity as with a waterfall project; instead, they give the team guard rails or areas to explore. By taking a breadth-first approach, the team can quickly gain an overall understanding of the solution. This approach doesn't exclude a deep dive establishing specific details if these are deemed too complicated or a little vague. Using a broad first approach also helps with estimation and particularly with the design to cost concepts outlined later.

Involving stakeholders in the modelling and documenting of their requirements is to be recommended. Not only can they quickly or succinctly provide clarifying information, but they also actively contribute towards the work as well. Sometimes requirements modelling or elucidation requires some training, mentoring and support from a coach, but the payback from this effort is often well worth the investment.

Why is this important? The business stakeholders are the subject matter experts, and as such, they fully understand the vision and objectives. The stakeholders know what they want, and if they can appreciate how to model and document requirements, this can be of long-term value. Collaboration in this way also makes sense because it distributes the modelling effort to more people and increases understanding.

Using a combination of requirements modelling with benefits mapping keeps the stakeholders focused on the achievement of the intended value from the activity.

The Benefits Mapping Recipe

Some teams struggle with defining their scope and breaking high-level requirements into detailed specifications. Sometimes, clarity can be achieved by getting stakeholders and team members to participate in a benefits mapping exercise. The mapping exercise may be part of a big room planning event or as a separate collaborative precursor.

Benefits Mapping is a process led by the product owners. Benefits Mapping is one of the main tools used in benefits management. It is also a means of visually depicting the links between the activities, identifying deliverables and establishing the desired business outcomes.

The resultant map is a guide which shows where the value and benefits of the activity lie. A benefits map can describe:

- The necessary solution requirements are linked to the business outcomes, and therefore the meeting of business objectives.
- The activities needed to deliver facilities or technologies required to enable further changes. In this instance, it will map these enablers linking them to the business changes, and finally business benefits or desired outcomes.
- For activities requiring more than one initiative, a benefits map will show how the interdependencies build across a programme or portfolio, showing enabling technical capabilities, business capabilities, building up to the business outcomes, which are required in total to meet the overall objectives.

Benefits mapping can be used at the portfolio management level and at the initiative level to identify the high-level components in a backlog. A significant advantage of the benefits map is that it helps a large team to formulate how the business value is created in the work they are doing.

Due to its visual nature, it's quite easy to trace all the actions leading up to a goal. On more significant activities, deliverables and responsibilities can be divided between component and feature teams using the benefits map. In this, any assumptions that made during the mapping exercise become explicit and can be challenged, during the big room planning sessions.

Benefits Mapping Ingredients

From a coaching perspective, benefits mapping is a simple technique to master. For a description of the method, see the Benefits Management section of Managing Successful Programmes[xiv]. Once the team understands benefits mapping, then a coach is likely to use a facilitating style of intervention. Most teams understand the technique very quickly and therefore, in this context, once training is complete, a mentoring form of intervention is often unnecessary for the coach.

The principle of the benefits map is that it allows the team and stakeholders to visualise how the initiatives, the technical and business capabilities and business outcomes relate to the strategic goal.

In the example below, the strategic objective is to increase profit by £650,000 by improving the service provided to customers. The agile initiative has three features: a new service process supported by a new software tool and a lean activity which designs a new target operating model. The map shows from a benefits perspective how the features and the benefits are linked. It allows a team to work from right to left across the entire map to evaluate the contribution from each component deliverable will make towards the whole.

As the features decompose into work items, epics and stories, if required, additional detail can be added to the map to establish the value delivered during each iteration or sprint.

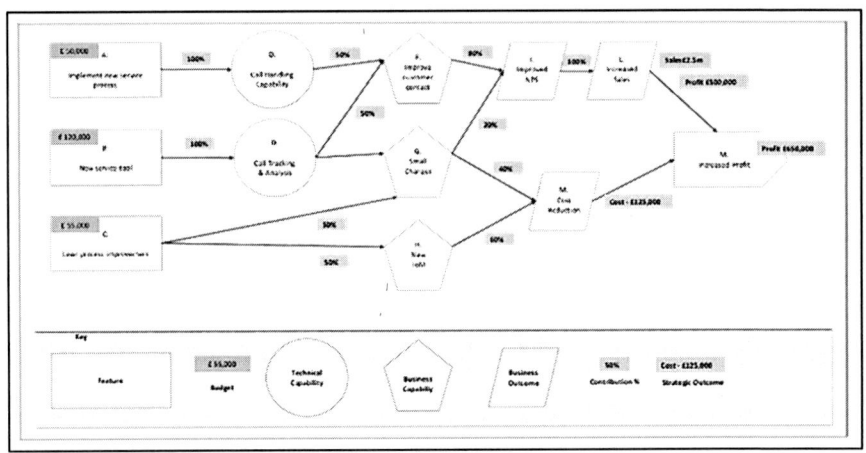

An example of a benefits map

Linking the benefits from the mapping exercise to the work items enables backlog refinement. If an epic appears on the backlog without an associated value, it will cause a team to question why it is requested.

Sprint Backlog Refinement

Product backlog refinement or management is when the team and product owner discuss the top priority items remaining on the product backlog. During backlog refinement, the team asks questions that if unanswered would need clarification during individual sprint or demand planning. If questions clarifying the work appear first time in sprint planning, it could be disruptive. Sometimes the questions result in the product owner needing to seek clarification from stakeholders or subject matter experts.

Further, if answers are not forthcoming for too many requirements, then it may be necessary to put high-priority work items on one side. The questions thereby delay the inclusion of these work items in the delivery process until they can be clarified. By giving the team a chance of asking these questions earlier, the product owner can establish the answers to queries he or she may not be prepared to answer immediately.

Questions raised do not need entirely resolved in a product backlog refinement meeting. Instead, the product owner needs only to address them just enough so that the team feels confident that the work item can be discussed and estimated during the upcoming Sprint planning meeting.

Some coaches focus on the correct use of the user story syntax for work items in the backlog. The goal has never been that an entire product backlog should be written as user stories. The goal has not been to have everything on a product backlog written with "As a… I want… So that…" The goal is to have a product backlog – a list that represents the known, needed work items; some of these will be tasks, some stories and some epics.

Sprint Backlog Refinement Recipe

As part of the tailoring process, the definition of ready will set by each team, or potentially a standard definition across several teams, if they are working on a single product release. This definition sets the standard that all requirements should meet before epics and stories included in a sprint plan. This definition of ready assists backlog management by:

- Allowing an assessment of a work items status – the "ready" state.
- Keeping the roles in the team accountable to each other; the product owner to the team, and the team to the Scrum Master.
- Helping the team identify when the product owner or another team member becomes overwhelmed. The symptoms are many unprepared work items.
- Reducing the pressure on the team to commit to estimates before stories are "Ready".
- Ensuring that the stories that enter a sprint can be completed due to no surprises arising when completing the work.
- Allowing stakeholders to have had a chance to input into the requirement.

The backlog preparations or story refinement sessions are used by the product owner and team to improve the quality of the backlog and prepare items so that they may be worked on and completed. Its purpose is to understand the requirements entirely or to refine stories and acceptance criteria through splitting. In this activity, stories are prioritised, estimated and prepared the backlog to ensure productive Sprint and Release planning. This activity may happen as part of the product owner's actions or as a small-group or whole team exercise.

Signs that the team may be showing insufficient attention to backlog refinement include:

1. Lengthy conversations about the requirement during sprint planning – sometimes product owners may try to cut corners or have inadequate data themselves about what is truly needed.
2. Requirements "churn" in development – i.e. adding items and deleting items during the Sprint.
3. Reworking – A story without proper information may be the cause of rework or defects, or worse create items which are waste. That is, identified as having taken completely wrong direction during the Sprint Review at worst.
4. Stories in the backlog without tests or clearly defined acceptance criteria.

Kanban Backlog Management

Every initiative, product or service starts with a list of requirements. The Kanban backlog is a means of avoiding chaos and providing order in the process of delivering value to customers.

According to Lean, maintaining a prioritised backlog is waste. It is seen as waste because the effort of continually prioritising work items which may never be started is pointless. Consequently, requested work items are prioritised according to rules and then slotted into the right place in the backlog.

The Kanban backlog rules relate to the type of work, the numbers of WIP items, the process flow and the priority. For example, an emergency defect fix may have a "stop all work and swarm" rule. An item with a fixed end date (for regulatory reasons) could have a "must start by rule".

Kanban Backlog Management Recipe

The Kanban backlog consists of a list of requested work items. Each requirement identifies the potential customer value and the desired outcome. Each work item has its importance in the pool of available work and confirms clear objectives.

It is typical for this backlog, a list of requested items to be visually displayed on a board which is separate from the main Kanban board. As new requests arrive from customers, these work items are added to the backlog list. Likewise, if a business requirement changes or if the team receives additional feedback, some work items become more important than others (the rules change). This backlog must be adjusted to reflect those changes in priority. To properly rank and prioritise each work item, a classification the Class of Service (COS) is used. The COS enables work items to be grouped, prioritised and facilitates decision-making. For example, if too many work items of one COS are on the backlog, or in-flight, that may or may not be a cause for concern. The Service Request Manager clarifies and explores each request in the same way as the product owner refines the backlog in Scrum, completing the necessary details to enable the team to progress.

Once all the details are complete, a team pulls work from the Backlog into the "To-Do" area of the Kanban, typically during the regular Replenishment meeting. Then when a work item moves into the "In Progress" area, this signifies that the team has committed to complete the item within the tolerances of a service level agreement.

From a coaching perspective, a developing Service Request manager will require as much support as a developing product owner. An additional coaching focus for Kanban is the rules. Clarifying the Kanban Rules and making them explicit and adhered to by a team is often needed. An immature team usually has difficulty in applying the WIP limits and coaching intervention is sometimes needed in the daily stand up.

Estimation Recipes

Estimating the work in an agile initiative is fundamentally different from traditional project methods of estimation. From a coaching point of view, this difference presents a challenge until the team master this new "black" art!

It may be useful to recap why an estimate, irrespective of whether the team plans to use Scrum or Kanban. The main reason for sizing features, epics and user stories is so that the team can commit to iteration goals, plan releases and prioritise work. When they know the size of work items and the team's delivery performance, a team can then approximate the time of deliveries of features to the customer. The main reason for estimating is to be able to decide on an appropriate workload for each sprint.

The traditional estimating approach is to use a "bottom-up" technique: where the team details out all requirements and estimates each task needed to complete those requirements in hours or days. A project manager then uses this data to develop the project schedule. Agile activities, in contrast, typically use a "top-down" approach, using high-level estimation techniques for Features or Epics, then employing progressive elaboration or rolling-wave planning methods during sprint or demand planning to drill down into the detail and task level estimates on a just-in-time basis.

The traditional waterfall estimating causes projects is to spend several weeks or months at the beginning of the activity, collecting detailed requirements. For an agile fixed price activity, exact specifications similar to those used in a waterfall activity may be necessary. For target price contracts and time and materials activities, detailing requirements upfront is generally not required.

The organisational context of the activity-funding model generally dictates the level of constraint and degree of control which should be practised by an agile team. For example, fixed price, fixed time, agile initiatives need stronger controls than time and material activities.

Some initiatives need to use a Design-to-Cost approach coupled with MoSCoW[xv] requirements prioritisation to provide restraints on cost. Other activities may have a greater emphasis on fulfilling the requirement, regulatory activities, for example. In regulatory activities, the control emphasis is more around requirements management and the time-to-market than the budget. The agile coach needs to be aware of these differences and coach each team accordingly.

Agile has a variety of estimation and control techniques available, and it will depend upon the type of activity, the organisational culture and the experience of the team as to which is most appropriate.

Some agilists infer that estimation is not needed and the work completed when done. However, there are not many organisations who can tolerate this stance from a corporate governance perspective. I have therefore included a design-to-cost technique as part of this section so that coaches may give guidance to teams working within budgetary constraints.

The Initial Estimation Recipe

In waterfall, estimation models almost set out the complete project plan from conception through to project closure. In agile, we create that plan this is based upon the high-level requirements – the release plan – the MVP with any subsequent releases. Then the team aligns the plan and adjusts the estimates of work to be completed based upon the recently completed activities.

Agile estimation techniques either rely heavily upon team-based estimation often referred to as the "wisdom of crowds" or they rely on past data as in Kanban. Either of which means that the agile coach is involved in initially training then mentoring and finally facilitating the team estimation activities.

Planning Poker, for example, is a wisdom of the crowd's technique known as a wideband Delphi. These wisdom techniques use four generic principles.

Principles	Description
Diversity of understanding	Each person should understand the requirement hence the discussions regarding the scope and range of the work to be completed based upon known facts.
Independence	The individual's opinions aren't determined by the views of those around them. (Hence the use of Poker Cards.)
Decentralisation	People are specialist and can draw on their specific experience and knowledge.
Aggregation	The mechanism for turning individual private judgments into a collective team decision.

T-shirt Sizing Recipe

The initial agile estimation technique often used by teams is T-shirt sizing. The T-shirt sizing is a ratio or weighting of the expected work to produce a feature or epic.

During the early stages, the team participates in discovery workshops with the customer to further understand the work to be completed. As each Feature or Epic is defined, it is estimated. This is to ensure that the work and time required can fit within the project commercial cost and time envelope.

Coaching estimation is often a prolonged period using mentoring style, requiring the coach to remind the teams of the principles and techniques of agile estimation. In estimation, teams often fall into bad habits, and they consequently need an often reminder of the basics.

T-shirt Sizing Ingredients

T-shirt Sizing involves classifying each feature and or Epic as being Small (S), Medium (M) or more significant (L, XL, XXL). This technique uses what is known as a relative value technique. Estimates are derived based upon the comparison, with a Large (L) being twice the size of an M and half the size of an XL. These values are not estimates but synthetic data which indicates the amount of work to be completed.

Size	Ratio
S	1
M	2
L	4
XL	8
XXL	16

If an item is too big, then it should be broken down by splitting the functional description until it can fit within the Small to the Extra-Extra-Large range. The calibration of the T-shirt sizes allows the application of the design-to-cost approach.

Kanban Estimation Recipe

Moving from Scrum to Kanban. Kanban doesn't prescribe a similar estimation and planning routine to Scrum. So how do Kanban teams' size work and plan release?

The question with Kanban is, do we need to estimate or not. In Kanban, the estimation of the anticipated time required to produce a work item is optional. After a work item is completed, the team members pull the next item from the backlog and proceed with implementing it. Some teams are required to carry out estimation to provide predictability to their stakeholders. One alternative approach to achieve predictability is to make sure that each of the work items is approximately the same size, and therefore can most likely be completed in the same amount of time.

This approach removes the need to estimate each task in detail. However, an expectation of how much time is needed is often required. Instead, throughput is calculated by taking the number of work items of a particular class of service delivered in a certain period.

And to calculate total time to release, we can use Little's Law. Little's Law is basic queue theory, defining the relationship between Work in Progress (WIP), Throughput and Lead Time.

Kanban Control Ingredients

Kanban control is determined by rules associated with a Class of Service (CoS) and the calculation of lead time and cycle time. A CoS, for example, may relate to a feature, or an emergency fix, or a type of data migration activity. The CoS rules allow a team to estimate, based upon cycle time and probability, how much time is likely to be required to complete each work item. Kanban cycle time tracks the average time taken for each CoS. It allows the team to assess the probability of completing any task within a project within a defined time frame.

While cycle time can assess team delivery efficiency, it can also predict likely future performance. Cycle time scatterplots provide a visual method to estimate task times and quickly identify problem areas. Reducing average cycle times means higher team productivity, faster delivery, increased customer satisfaction.

While Kanban cycle time is calculating the actual work-in-progress time, the lead-time is the time between a request arriving from a customer and its' completion. It is total time that the customer is waiting for delivery. Lead-time may also be broken down into several cycle times relating to the different process stages.

The Design to Cost Recipe

During solution development, the agile team must address factors such as product; features, cost, performance, schedule or time-to-market and quality. The importance of these factors depend upon organisational context and may vary from product to product or market to market.

Yet what happens if the estimates in terms of cost or time exceed the potential budget allocated or provided to deliver the solution? Budgets are not limitless, and sooner or later, they are all exhausted. I have found that the answer lies in a systems engineering technique known as design-to-cost. The benefit of the design-to-cost approach is that it recognises the solution features deliver customer benefits and these are aligned with the budget constraints. It is a technique used by manufacturers in nearly every product design process, from cars to cell phones.

Most organisations use some form of high-level product breakdown to list out the features and to establish their target price or budget for the solution. This list of features is then used to breakdown the solution budget so that each feature has a nominal budget allocation. The design-to-cost technique ensures that the essential revenue or beneficial features have enough budget or time allocation to ensure their completion. The design-to-cost approach uses the team estimation of likely work to be completed to assess design choices with the cost objectives in mind. The two factors benefit and potential cost loosely provide a return-on-investment type picture of each feature. It causes the team to challenge expenditure on features with little or no anticipated benefit to focus on features with significant benefits.

Design-to-cost considers the financial constraints and commitments to the customer in benefit terms while the project is in the Inception or during the requirement detailing activities. In this way, the risk of potential for cost and schedule overruns are controlled or at least limited from the outset. In cases where additional budget is required, then the team has the estimated data necessary to support this request.

Design to Cost Ingredients

Design to cost uses the target budget for the total activity and divides this by the required product features according to their T-shirt sizing. The calculation gives a target budget per feature, which is balanced against the expected benefits.

The target budget provides a cost ceiling so that the product owners and stakeholders can make design choices based upon the potential benefit and anticipated cost per feature. Additional data may be provided by linking the target cost profile with the solution benefits map. In this way, the team can establish if the anticipated effort involved in delivering the next feature is justified by the anticipated additional benefit.

As features are decomposed into work items, the team ensures that the sum of the estimates for the work items does not exceed the budget for the feature. If the budget is exceeded, then the team either revised the design or seeks to take some budget from another feature. If the budget cannot be balanced, then the feature with the lowest benefit is deprived of funding until further funding can be found.

Design to cost principles can also be used in the Kanban context where the average lead-time and therefore cost per work item can be used to anticipate reaching the budgetary ceiling. (This would be a different calculation per class of service.)

Agile Risk Management Recipe

Some suggest that merely by being an agile endeavour; this somehow reduces the need for further Risk Management. Risks, irrespective of the project delivery method, should be explicitly managed. An agile coach needs to be well versed in the application of agile risk management.

The critical underlying principle is simple; as the level of risk associated with the delivery of a project falls, then the probability of a successful outcome increases.

As everyone wishes to be associated with a successful activity, I recommend that risk management is an essential element of all projects irrespective of the delivery process. It is recommended that Risk Management should be undertaken in a Lean manner; avoiding wasted effort. Risk management should happen during release planning, refined during sprint planning and monitored during the sprint review.

It is important to stress that risk management is an art form, not a science, and its purpose is to reduce the time a team may spend "firefighting" should problems be encountered. There is always a trade-off; will a team spend more time managing a risk, or firefighting should that problem occur? Pragmatically, the team could opt to firefight low impact-low probability risks should they happen. Risks with high impact-high probability the team will want to avoid or take mitigating action. The team's balance between the management of risks and firefighting needs to be respected and encouraged by the coach. Firefighting distracts the team. It reduces delivery efficiency and causes delays.

In projects or programmes, there are typically two kinds of risks; delivery risks and business risks, the same is true of agile activities.

Delivery risks are those scenarios which may happen and if they occur could be harmful to the successful outcome of the initiative, budget or timeline. Once prepared, the risk responses result in an improved risk profile. The Sponsor indicates that the resultant risk profile acceptable, i.e. within their risk appetite, and the team are good to go! The risks will be recorded in a risk register or log though the team may decide that some other mechanism is more appropriate, and the mitigating actions will be added to the product backlog.

The business risks are the risks which the business manages typically using an enterprise risk management framework. Sometimes these risks are also called operational risks. In changing, or introducing, new processes or products, the business needs to apply control mechanisms so that it does not encounter business risks such as; inadvertent damage its reputation, fraud, negative impact to customers or breaches legislation or regulations. In assessing the effects on business risks, the initiative will identify the need for revised or new operational controls and potential key risk indicators. New business risks will often need to be recorded in the Enterprise Risk Register, and the Controls and Risk Indicators implemented as part of the project before the go-live activities.

Fundamentally, the sponsor owns the business risks. The business risk owners make use of the organisation's business risk management processes to address any changes on behalf of the sponsor.

Agile Risk Management Ingredients

In either Scrum or Kanban, identifying and monitoring delivery risk levels are the concern of the whole team. Risks are managed using a process called PRAM[xvi] (Project Risk Analysis and Management). Under PRAM; Risks are Identified, Evaluated, a response is prepared, then the ongoing risk level is monitored.

Risk identification happens at several points in an agile project. During release planning, and they are refined (evaluated, and probability and impact reassessed) during sprint planning. During solution or sprint reviews, the current risk profile is also considered. During the Scrum, new risks can be identified. Hence, project risk management should happen almost continuously, yet it is often a forgotten element for a lot of agile teams.

The process is, of course, entirely subjective as the team are trying to define a "future possible event". Through clearly outlining the risk in the first place, the team makes educated assumptions and estimates. This allows provision to be prepared for with greater accuracy and degrees of confidence. The more precise they can be the better, but if they have a figure, it is much more useful than purely rating them as red, amber or green.

The benefit of using a systematic – albeit subjective – approach to risk management is that it encourages the team to insert mitigation activities into the backlog to reduce overall initiative risk levels. It focuses the attention of the team on why these mitigation activities are needed and to help the follow-through to ensure the risk mitigation has the desired result.

Risk	Probability	Impact	Weighting X 100	Resolution Date
Risk A	10%	3	30	Sprint 1
Risk B	5%	2	10	Sprint 2
Risk C	10%	1	10	Sprint 3
Risk D	10%	1.5	15	Sprint 4
Risk E	5%	2	10	Sprint 5
Risk F	15%	2	30	Sprint 7
Total			120	

Risk Log or Table

The approach uses a combination of risk impact and probability. The impact is a judgement of the size of the effect on the activity should the risk scenario occur. The impact of the occurrence of a risk is rated on a scale. For example, One to Five. Where one is very low, two is low, three is medium, four is high and five very high. The probability is a subjective guess as to the likelihood of the problem occurring, often judged on a percentage scale. When multiplied together, impact times probability, this formula gives a risk weighting or risk value. The weighting provides a mechanism whereby risks can be classified, monitored and mitigating actions prioritised.

The impact is usually assessed in terms of time (schedule delays) and cost (additional project expense). If possible, real values should be assigned to potential impacts to quantify them. If the risk has been defined in terms of a cause, impact relationship, where the effect relates to a specific work package, milestone or deliverable, then the team can quickly start to drill down on the risk to try to assess what the impact could be and what would be the probability occurrence.

The delivery risk weighting is expressed as the potential negative impact on the project. The higher the weighting, the more significant is the risk. The probability and impact factors are reassessed after the risk mitigation actions or risk response. This expression is often called the nett or residual risk weighting.

Risk weightings are tagged to epics, stories or spikes and during release planning these are allocated into sprints or a release or programme integration point.

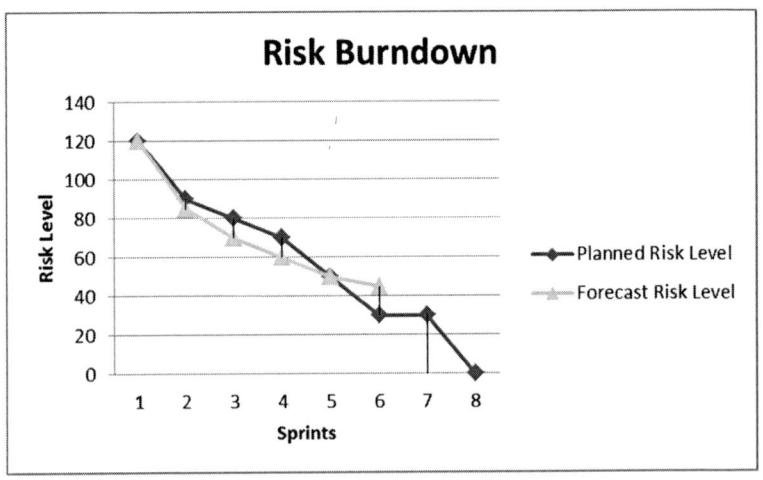

Risk Burndown showing planned and forecast levels

The result is that each risk with its risk weighting will be associated with a sprint or release endpoint. When the sprint concludes, with the completion of the epic, story or feature, then the risks no longer exist. The result is that the level of delivery risk has fallen and thus can be displayed as a risk burndown chart as shown. The completion of a sprint or release point will reduce the weighting of those risks associated with completed user stories to zero.

During the sprint review, the team should, as a matter of process, evaluate the result of the sprint on the delivery risk profile. However, the sprint review may also identify new risks or that the probability of occurrence of a risk in the future should be changed. The result can also be mapped in the risk burndown chart as forecast risk levels, as shown in the risk burndown.

In the example, the risk profile of the project at the end of Sprints 2, 3 and 4 are better than initially planned though at the end of Sprint 6, the level is above the original plan. The profile could be due to the team planning to defer the completion of a story with associated risks from Sprint 2 until Sprint 6, for example.

The evaluation of risk enables mitigation actions or contingency plans to be adequately defined, where the probability of a risk is judged to be between 10% and 60%, either these risks depending upon impact will have mitigation actions or a contingency plan drawn up.

A probability of less than 10% can be considered unlikely to happen, and therefore no further action is needed. If greater than 60%, then the activity needs to be examined thoroughly.

Mitigation has the effect of reducing either the probability or impact of a risk, sometimes both. The team should track the resultant risk values after reduction by mitigation to give an accurate picture of the level of uncertainty involved in their activity.

Delivery risks are typically associated with a specific; epic, story, or programme integration point. The epics, stories and tasks are planned into the sprints. The planned mitigation actions appear in the sprint backlogs as risk spikes. A spike is a fixed point; as such, it is a mandatory task required at a certain point in time.

Release Planning Recipe

The foundation of every successful activity is the planning. While an agile plan is significantly different from a traditional project schedule, this statement is still very much applicable. The planning process allows teams to think through how they plan to succeed and in doing so, they create a flexible, agile plan.

It is also right to say that not all agile plans are the same. For example, a plan which may be appropriate for an exploratory product activity is unlikely to be acceptable for an agile project delivering regulatory compliance. The agile coach needs to apply judgement to ensure that the level and detail in the planning is appropriate for the organisational context and provide mentoring or training if it is not.

A release plan acts as a map; it provides the context of the deliveries and the direction based upon the goals, vision and expectations for the product. According to the PMI, the most common cause of project failure is unclear scope requirements. So, for product owners, nailing the solution or product goals before the initial planning is crucial. Yet there is nothing to stop these goals being developed, enhanced or removed in the future – that's the nature of agile!

Agile release planning is an approach to scheduling which considers the intangible and flexible nature of development. Agile; teams plan sprints iteratively across incremental releases. In other words, instead of trying to develop every proposed feature at the same time in one large, orchestrated project, agile breaks down the delivery process into time boxes called sprints and releases. Releases are mostly time-periods built up of several sprints defined to deliver a limited set of the functions of the overall project. An agile release plan sets out how and when features will be released and delivered to customers.

Release Planning Ingredients

Agile release planning is a highly structured process. Each step carefully detailed and measured to create high-level project calendars for teams to follow, amend and adjust as work progresses.

Release plans will vary depending on the size of the team, the nature of the activities; the number of workstreams and, so on, but the general elements will include:

- The proposed number of release(s) for the project
- Planned features for each release or iteration
- Features to be delivered in subsequent iterations
- Activities to develop features within a release
- Individual tasks to prepare for or complete the release

This level of release planning is combined with a time-boxed schedule, the sprint or iteration plan; to give the dynamic nature and flexibility which in agile product development so valuable.

Agile Testing Recipes

Agile ways of working require a depth of continuous collaboration between stakeholders that are uncommon in a traditional project delivery process. In agile, testing becomes an essential component at every phase of the developmental process. The emphasis is to "baked in" product quality at every stage of its development.

In agile testing, compared to a traditional approach, there are few detailed requirements documents and functional checklists. Instead, using test-driven techniques, the agile team defines tests and then builds the requirement. The agile goal is to create the solution to pass a test which will satisfy a customer's request.

The team will have replaced up-front detailed documentation with in-person meetings, and therefore agile project specification has fewer artefacts for rigid QA processes to use. Yet a fixation on the quality of the solution delivered is a fundamental agile principle.

A second factor is the role of people in an agile self-organising project team. In the agile culture, everyone works closely together, no matter his or her part, to achieve a single goal. Which is a high-quality solution which fulfils the agreed essential specifications the stakeholders require with each iteration.

Agile Testing Ingredients

From a coaching perspective, it is highly desirable to see a team being explicit about their approach to quality. During agile process, tailoring the team should consider the appropriate measures and techniques they plan to use to deliver an excellent solution. Their approach to quality involves typically:

- A test strategy and plan.
- The use of appropriate techniques.
- Environments and tooling.
- Applied metrics for assurance.

Having established the foundations for quality, the team needs diligence in the application, and sometimes this requires intervention from a coaching perspective.

Test Planning Recipe

Agile initiatives consider quality from the outset. Poor quality increases waste and slows down the delivery process. Agile, therefore, has at its core a "right-first-time" ethic using specific agile quality assurance techniques.

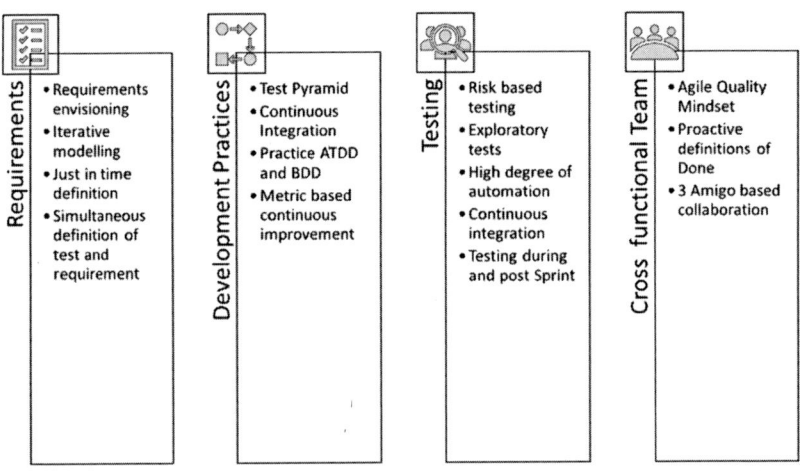

Agile Quality Assurance Principles

Quality assurance is defined as *"the planned and systematic approach to the evaluation of the quality of and adherence to product standards, processes and procedures"*. This systematic approach is quite different in agile and traditional environments. Quality in the Agile context is the result of empirical control; relying on the three fundamental ideas of transparency, inspection and adaptation.

Transparency starts with the definition of requirements in the context of what is likely to be accepted by testing. Inspection is focussed on the development practices and concluded with continuous integration. The adaptation is a result of the team checking their interpretation of the requirements with their stakeholders and adjusting based upon the feedback.

Often the feedback must be balanced with the commercial context of the activity. In some instances, this may lead to the ubiquitous waterfall-like change control process. However, this is some team's reality no matter how this is frowned upon by some agile purists.

Quality at the team level then starts with gaining clarity over the vision and requirements and uses techniques and tools to deliver the desired results. At the enterprise, level quality is about the provision of an agile ecosystem which allows teams to thrive.

The team-based quality plan should lever a whole team approach establishing the delivery practices or mechanisms at the iteration and the release levels. It is also about the testing techniques and tools which will be used by the team to assure solution quality.

Lastly, quality is also about the functioning of the team, the application of the agile mindset, the team roles and responsibilities and the approach to ensuring that an excellent solution is delivered. This view of excellence is backed up by the team's use of metrics to monitor their progress.

Test Plan Ingredients

According to the International Software Testing Qualifications Board, a test plan is a document which describes the scope, approach, resources and schedule of testing activities.

In the agile context, the team is responsible for testing the solution, and the test plan provides a means if required to illustrate to those outside the team that adequate quality measures have been undertaken. The organisation is responsible for the provision of a delivery ecosystem which is supportive of the team goals.

Unlike a traditional teat plan, an agile test plan is written and updated for each iteration and aligns to the release plan. The agile test plan indicates the type of testing performed in each iteration. It outlines test data and environment requirements and the level of automation used.

Test-driven recipe

A test-driven approach is just one of the many agile collective terms used. It embraces several techniques so; understandably, people can get confused. Typically, when talking about using a test-driven approach, people could be referring to:

- Acceptance Test-Driven Development (ATDD)
- Behaviour-Driven Development (BDD)
- Test-Driven Development (TDD)
- Continuous Testing
- Model-Based Testing (MBT)

The following guidelines are provided for any test-driven approach

It should communicate clearly	As test driven-development used as a technique where the test in-part defines the requirement. It is, therefore, essential that the test is understood by all involved.
Should provide meaningful feedback	Testing is expensive in terms of time taken by the agile team. The test, therefore, needs to be able to add value to the development activity
The test should be reliable	TDD helps the team to avoid duplicating of code as the team. It tests a small amount of system at a time building up to system and solution tests. Such tests need to be able to be repeated and give a result on which the team can rely.
Easy to maintain	The basis of TDD is the repetition of tests the development grows. It is therefore essential that the tests themselves have a low cost of ownership. For the team to be able to increment the testing, as the delivery of the solution progresses.

Software developers, testers and quality-assurance personnel all wear each other's hats from time to time. While there may be a group of people running most of the tests, the notion of a separate testing team almost disappears entirely. Yet this is not a given and may change team-to-team and sprint-to-sprint. It is this collaborative dimension to the agile approach the team deciding who is going to do the work, that people believe sets it apart from other methods.

Acceptance Test-Driven Development Recipe

Acceptance Test-Driven Development (ATDD) involves the team with a different set of perspectives (usually customer-orientated). Using ATDD, the team collaborates with Stakeholders to write acceptance tests in advance of implementing the corresponding functionality.

The discussion that occurs to generate the ATDD tests is known as the "three amigos". The three amigos are perspectives representing; the Customer, what problem is the team trying to solve? Development, how might they solve this problem? And Quality Assurance what about testing the XYZ?

The ATDD tests represent the user's point of view and act to formulate the requirements. Describing how the system will function in addition to serving as a way of verifying that the system features as intended.

The Acceptance Test-Driven Ingredients

ATDD involves creating tests before code, and those tests represent expectations of the stakeholders that the solution should have. Using ATDD, the team creates one or more acceptance tests for each feature or Epic before beginning the delivery of the work item. Typically, the acceptance tests are discussed and captured when the team is working with stakeholders to scope the requirement. Acceptance criteria can also be collected as a by-product of a product owner outlining requirements during Backlog Preparation or Sprint Planning.

When captured, the test specification should be in a format supported by a functional test automation framework. The developers can then automate the tests by writing the supporting code ("fixtures"), as they implement the feature. The acceptance tests then become like executable requirements.

In trying ATDD, teams usually find that just the act of defining acceptance tests while discussing requirements results in improved stakeholder and team understanding of the business need. The ATDD test definition enables the team and subject matter experts to come to a concrete agreement about the exact solution behaviour required.

Teams that follow ATDD process all the way through, automating the tests as they implement the feature, typically find that the resulting software is more testable, the tests result in greater coverage and additional automated tests are relatively easy to add as the product is incrementally developed. Further, the resulting automated regression tests provide valuable, fast feedback about business-expectations. ATDD is strongly associated with the use of specific tools such as Fit, FitNess, Cucumber or others.

A risk, however, is that the availability of appropriate tooling. Lack of suitable tools will hinder rather than enable the goals of ATDD. The use of the tool should be adapted to meet product owner's needs rather than adapting ATDD to fit the tooling constraints.

Behaviour Driven Development Recipe

Behaviour Driven Development (BDD) is a refinement of the practices of Test-Driven Development (TDD) and Acceptance Test-Driven Development (ATDD). BDD augments TDD and ATDD in the following ways:

- Applying the "Five Whys" principle to each proposed, Feature, Epic and User Story, so that the outcome or purpose of each is clearly defined with regards to the definition of the desired business features,
- Only implementing those behaviours which contribute most directly to value generation, the required business outcomes, to minimise waste
- Describing the actions of a solution in a single notation which is directly accessible to domain experts, testers and developers, to improve communication.
- Applying these techniques down to the lowest levels of abstraction of the software, paying attention to the distribution of behaviour, so that evolution remains cheap.

Test-driven Development Recipe

Test-driven development (TDD) is used by software engineers to unit test a solution during construction. TDD encourages the developer to focus on product requirements before writing code. A fundamental shift from traditional programming where generally developers write unit tests after writing the code.

It is a process which relies on the testing of small increments of code in short development cycles using particular test cases. As the test cases are passed, then the software is improved, so that solution quality is ensured. TDD automation scripts as used extensively during the refactoring process.

TDD focuses on the "inside-out" perspective, meaning that tests are created from a developer's perspective. "Is this code correct?" is typically the driving question behind TDD. TDD focuses specifically on "unit tests". The developer takes a requirement and then converts it into a specific test case.

Continuous Testing Recipe

The old way of testing a solution used the V-model and the principle that the builder should not be the person who does the checks. The software was therefore handed from one team member to another for testing. A traditional project would, in theory, have separated development and QA phases. QA teams always wanted more time to ensure quality the developers more time to build. Philosophically, it was often thought that the goal was that the product quality should prevail over the schedule. In practice, however, this was rarely the case.

With agile, organisations want faster delivery of solutions to the market or the end-user. The newer the software, the better it can be marketed and used to increase revenue potential. Hence, a new way of testing aligned with the continuous delivery concept has evolved known as continuous testing.

Continuous Testing is defined as a type of software testing which involves testing early and often. It consists of examining the integrated solution using extensive test automation. Continuous Testing is an approach for evaluating quality at every step of the continuous delivery process.

Model-based Testing (MBT) Recipe

Model-based Testing is a software testing technique where the behaviour of the software under test is checked against predictions made by a model. It is not appropriate for all solutions. However, a model is developed which describes the system's response in certain situations. The required behaviour is defined in terms of input sequences, actions, conditions, outputs or the flow of data from input to output. The model should be practical, understandable, reusable, shared. The model provides an accurate description of the system to be tested. There are numerous types of models available; they are used to describe different aspects of the system behaviour. Examples of the model are:

- Data Flow
- Control Flow
- Dependency Graphs
- Decision Tables
- State Transition Machines

Model-based Testing offers significant benefits, such as increased accuracy. Improvement of test coverage, reduction of testing effort and improvement of quality. MBT offers a wide variety of techniques and capabilities that may appear overwhelming to initial adopters.

Model-Based Testing describes how a system should behave in response to an action (determined by a model). Supply the effect, and see, if the system responds as per the prediction. It is a lightweight testing method used to validate solution performance. This type of testing can be applied to both hardware and software testing.

Applied Test Metrics Recipe

Testing has an essential metric orientation, and the parameters to be used will be identified in the test plan. Yet, the agile philosophy is not to measure the testing itself, or the tester progress. Instead, agile measures test throughput, the output, the achievement of the iteration goal, as the primary data points.

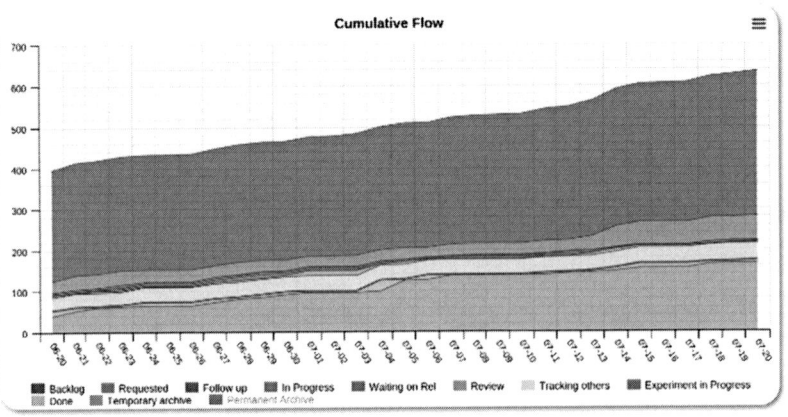

Cumulative Flow Diagram produced by Kanbanize

Irrespective of the testing approach from a coach's perspective, the key is to analyse the test metrics. Testing is a classic area where a cumulative flow diagram (CFD) should be applied and used for analysis. The CFD is a crucial instrument in queuing theory and mirrors the burn-up chart in some ways showing the quantity of work in each state. Agile teams should produce a quality CFD at the end of each Sprint and discuss this chart along with their Risk Matrix and velocity charts during the Sprint Review. Of course, as illustrated if the team is using Kanban, then the CFD can be used as a diagnostic of the whole project activities, not just the tests.

Activity Control Recipe

According to the PMI *"Project Controls are the data gathering, management and analytical processes used to predict, understand and constructively influence the time and cost outcomes of a project or program; through the communication of information in formats that assist effective management and decision making"*.[xvii] – Control comprises tracking performance against agreed plans and taking the corrective action required to meet the defined objectives. In agile, it is the manifestation of PDCA. Work is planned, done, progress monitored, metrics gathered and the team adjusts according to the data that they have collected. Sometimes, agile teams use either Scrum or Kanban or a combined process Scrum Ban.

From a coaching perspective, control is all about the predictability of the team. The agile coach needs to establish if adequate agile control principles are being applied. If the team is not predictable, then diagnosis needs to be undertaken, and the coach needs to target an intervention to improve control. Depending upon the issues and the diagnostic made, coaching interventions in the area of project control could use all the intervention styles, with the possible exception of professional coaching.

Activity Control Ingredients

Experience has shown that there is a sequence to the project control diagnosis, which can be applied by the coach.

1. Have the risks been appropriately identified and mitigated? – Check the risk log and determine that the mitigation actions are in the backlog or have been completed.
2. Has the team created a release plan which matches their commitments made to the customer? Is that release plan feasible and dynamic? Has the future been re-planned based upon the performance of the past?
3. Do the metrics produced by the team in terms of; time, quality and cost, when applied to the future indicate that the team will achieve the goals? If not, what corrective actions are planned?

The type of intervention required from the coach will depend on the severity of the control challenge and the maturity of the team.

Managing Activities Using Scrum Recipe

I have assumed that most readers of this book will be familiar with, if not master practitioners of Scrum. However, just in case, Scrum is a framework which helps teams to work together, yet it is primarily a means of project control, illustrating progress and increasing productivity. Scrum encourages teams to learn through experiences, self-organise while working on a problem and reflect on their wins and losses to continuously improve

Many teams practising "false agile" do so by going through the Scrum routines without adequately engaging with the basics of the techniques. An example of fake agile would be that the team hold a daily stand-up but do not calculate any metrics. When entirely used, Scrum increases team productivity and reduces delivery time when compared to classic "waterfall" processes. An agile Scrum process should benefit the organisation by:

- Improving the quality of the solution.
- Enabling adaption when changes occur (and allow for expected changes).
- Providing better estimates with an efficient process.
- Better control of schedule and status.

Scrum starts with backlog preparation leading to the sprint-planning meeting. Sprint-planning is used by the team to plan and make a commitment to what they will achieve in the next sprint. During Sprint-planning, the team also agree on a sprint goal with the product owner for the upcoming and maybe subsequent immediate iterations.

The Scrum (the daily stand-up) is a team time-boxed fifteen to twenty-minute high-energy synchronisation and control meeting. During which a team understands their status against the sprint goal, what each of the team members is working on, and how these work items may impact others. Velocity is the critical metric for Scrum teams; to plan, target and measure performance.

A Sprint Review is about demonstrating the results from the work of the entire team: designers, developers and the product owner. It is all about what has been collectively achieved. The review is held at the end of every sprint. This where the team demonstrate the next increment of the product to be delivered.

A sprint review is not a meeting designed to criticise. Or for the team to take further wish list items as suggested improvements to the product. (Scrum has other processes for that.) If you refer to the sprint review as a "demo", it is most likely all that's happening is precisely that! Instead of a collaborative, "inspect, measure and-adapt" event, a demo is sometimes at best treated as a beauty parade; where the team may get a few congratulatory remarks before the meeting concludes.

From a coaching perspective, if sprint reviews don't cover what's remaining in the product backlog in terms of value, the stakeholders will be left in the dark about how much effort is still required to achieve the goals of the initiative. This is important as decisions can stop initiatives when they have reached sufficiency to increase organisational agility.

Adding new requirement requests also comes at a price. Without transparency regarding the impact of further demands, stakeholders are often surprised to learn how much work remains. In the absence of revised forecasts from the team, it is only with these types of discussion will the required degree of transparency be achieved.

What can you do about it? During the sprint review, the product owner should talk about the state of the backlog: How much work is left? How much additional work was added to the backlog since the last sprint review? How do these changes given the current sprint metrics affect the anticipated timeline and budget? Inappropriate detail in the backlog may require a coach to give specific support to a new or inexperienced product owner.

However, familiarity often leads agile coaches into corrupt Scrum practices. Becoming a Scrum Mom, for example, is a recurring theme with coaches and Scrum Masters who think they're doing an excellent job while achieving the opposite effect. The derogatory term "Scrum Mum" has been coined as an agile antipattern, although the issue often goes much further and deeper into aspects of team self-organisation, responsibility and control. The pattern is that the coach takes the role of a parent for the development team and this inhibits ownership and accountability in the team. Once into the "Scrum Mum" mode, it may be challenging to extract oneself. Gradually reducing responsibilities and encouraging the team to take these activities up is the main route forward.

Becoming the "go-for" or pamperer is another negative trait. The coach or Scrum Master may want to do anything that's needed to get the team to perform well – fixing hardware, booking or changing rooms, organising lunches or coffee and so on. Team members get used to absolving themselves or taking care of their necessities. Eventually, this approach gradually erodes the position of the Scrum Master or coach and reduces the ability to challenge the team constructively due to reduced credibility.

Another common misunderstanding is that the Scrum Master should bubble wrap the team, safely protected them from "the bad outside of the team world" so that developers can focus on writing software. Two separate issues have been created: Firstly, developers lack the interactions and understanding to figure out what's going on around them. Second, it creates another unhealthy behaviour – a coaching dependency.

There are several anti-agile behavioural patterns in the area of decision-making.

- In some situations, the coach or Scrum Master may decide to make decisions on behalf of the team. While it's valid that the Scrum Master to represent a decision that the team has already made, the coach or Scrum Master is not a decision-maker!

- When teams move to self-organisation, they may sometimes feel lost, because decisions previously made by others now lie within the remit of the team. They consequently may feel uncomfortable about this level of responsibility and may look to the coach or Scrum Master to fill this decisioning gap. In short, if the coach or Scrum Master picks up this managerial monkey, they inhibit team growth, stopping them from becoming truly agile.

- Developers may also ask the coach or Scrum Master to fetch a decision that rests elsewhere in the organisation. Picking up this task when the team plays the "we are too busy" or the "helpless child" cards results in the team ducking the agile value of "individuals and interactions over processes and tools" and should also be avoided.

In short, familiarity with Scrum may present the coach with unique and unexpected challenges which need careful attention.

Scrum Control Metrics Recipe

The use of metrics is Scrum is to ensure the predictable delivery of solutions to customers. Scrum has three types of metrics; a measure of value delivered to customers, measures of team efficiency and lastly measures of team health

Time to market is a standard metric used in both Scrum and Kanban, which indicates the time an initiative takes to start providing value to customers. The definition of a Sprint Goal in value terms is an optional part of the scrum framework. A Sprint Goal can answer four questions for the team: What is the value created in each Sprint? What does the team need to do to achieve the Sprint Goal? How will the team know that the goal is reached? When to cease work on the initiative because of a reduction in value delivered. When to stop work is the use of a return-on-investment metric.

The most commonly used team efficiency measure is velocity. Velocity is a measure of how much work has been completed by the team; this sprint, on average, in previous sprints. It can be expressed in story points or working hours and assists with the estimation of how much work can be accomplished in future sprints. Quality metrics are also a measure of team efficiency. From a coaching perspective, the ratio between commit and achieved per sprint is extremely interesting as illustrates a dimension of team maturity with estimation and planning.

Measuring team health involves periodically surveying a scrum team to obtain an indication of job satisfaction. Another measure of team health could be the frequency with which team members request a change of team.

Managing Activities Using Kanban Recipe

Kanban is one of the most popular methods in use by agile teams today. Kanban is a system which offers several advantages. Namely; the simplicity of task planning, the ability to increase output and use by teams of all sizes. It gets its name from its literary meaning – visual signalling.

Kanban, when compared to Scrum, has a simplified planning process based upon backlog prioritisation. Kanban is used to control flow and work in progress, thereby increasing productivity. Scrum recommends the development team to have between 5 to 9 members. Kanban does not come with size limitations and allowing team members to adjust to the complexity of the work. Kanban does not mean having massive teams suddenly becomes a great idea. All the reasons why the size of the Scrum is limited still apply to Kanban. However, from a coaching perspective, it could be that the team-size is just a factor with which you need to work.

Rather than as in Scrum work is managed according to time-boxed boundaries, Kanban reflects that the work progress flows continuously through a production system. Kanban is a widely used system to design and improve the flow of many types of work. It allows agile organisations to start activities with the existing workflow system and to drive evolutionary changes gradually. They can do this by reducing the size of work items, visualising their flow of work, limit work in progress (WIP) and stop starting work and start finishing work.

Kanban delivers shortened time cycles. Cycle time is the crucial metric for Kanban teams. Cycle time is calculated as the amount of time it takes for a work item to progress through the team's workflow – from the moment work starts to completion. By optimising cycle time, the team can confidently forecast the delivery of future work. Seeing the average cycle time drop in the control chart is an indicator of success for the team.

Kanban gives planning flexibility over Scrum. The focus of a team using Kanban is the work items in progress. Once the team completes a work item, they take the next work item off the top of the backlog. The Service Delivery Manager is free to reprioritise the backlog without disrupting the team because any changes outside of the current work in progress do not impact the team. If the product owner keeps the most important work items on top of the backlog, then the team is assured they continue to deliver the maximum business value. In this sense, there is no need for the fixed-sprint lengths found in Scrum. However, some Kanban teams mirror a fixed sprint cycle for planning, control and coordination purposes.

Kanban has no team size limitations and no set roles. Therefore, team members may continue to practice their traditional roles and responsibilities within the Kanban team. Also, Kanban allows individuals to gradually reduce commitments to more than one team becoming dedicated to one team over time. As such, it represents less of an immediate organisational change when compared to Scrum. However, this gradual adoption has significance for the coach. The gradual adoption should be reflected in the coaching plan and transformational road map so that productivity does not plateau, and continuous improvement is enabled.

Kanban has application from individual teams, through more substantial activities – programmes, to business level to the enterprise portfolio itself.

Kanban Work-in-Progress Limits Recipe

Many agile teams using Scrum use a Kanban board to visualise their work and control flow. Agile teams often talk about limiting work in progress; however, the reality is slightly different in that they forget. Adding a swim lane for each individual or applying an avatar to each work item on the Kanban board may be a means to draw attention to the fact that the team is breaking their rules in terms of WIP or some other agreement.

It is a Lean principle that multitasking kills efficiency. The more work items in flight at any given time, the more context switching the team encounters, which hinders the effectiveness of their path to completion. That's why a fundamental tenet of Kanban is to limit the amount of work in progress (WIP). A Kanban team without the scrutiny of their WIP limits is a cause for concern for an agile coach. Using the cumulative flow diagram visualises blockages and capacity constraints. Work-in-progress limits highlight bottlenecks and backups in the team's process due to lack of focus, people or skill sets.

Control in Kanban like Scrum relies upon mathematics. This maths starts with the estimation of work items. Some teams estimate while others prefer not to estimate at all! Still, others prefer to set a direction using roadmaps, like release plans, adding details to the map regularly so that they can assess progress. Yet the team context involves fixed deadlines and multi-team release dates then a certain amount of estimation is essential.

Estimates are by their definition are inexact and can be affected by many different risk factors. The Kanban method proposes data-driven, probability-based estimation using only historical performance records.

Kanban Control Metrics Recipe

The critical analysis tool used in Kanban is the cumulative flow diagram which shows a detailed picture of all stages in the delivery value chain. The Lead and Cycle Time Diagram represents the average amount of time for work item completion. It may also be used by a coach to measure improvements in performance.

Kanban metrics are used to help the team to assess; their delivery time, predictability, solution quality and the results of improvements. The following table is an example of some metrics used by Kanban teams.

	Work items completed	Defects
Definition	A daily count of the work items completed	A daily total of the team's unresolved defects
Kanban concept measurement	Average lead time for completed work items per day	The ratio between discovered and completed defects per day
Moving average of Kanban concept captures	Weekly velocity analysis – number of work items completed – team productivity	Product quality
Release predictability	The number of work items completed for the milestone or release date	Unresolved defects by day
Kanban calculation	Queue time as expressed by Little's Law	The average time taken for defect resolution

Of course, this is not an exhaustive list. If the team size is a variable, then specific metrics will need to be divided by the number of team members to obtain a consistent picture. Any moving averages should be based on a seven-day (weekly) or thirty-days (monthly) period.

Continuous Improvement

Continuous, relentless improvement is a principle of Lean. Scrum uses the retrospective as a means of improving productivity. In Kanban, the Service Delivery Review mirrors the Scrum Retrospective with the same agenda.

With being a self-managed team, those individuals also take on the responsibility for self and team improvement. We are talking hard facts, productivity or efficiency rarely is this about people or relationships unless this impact the hard facts.

When coaching a team in the principles of continuous improvement, the coach needs facts. This involves the collection of data diagnosis over time so that the coach may point to particular trends. The coaching-style again will depend upon the maturity of the team but is likely to focus on the facilitating style.

Sprint Retrospective Recipe

In general terms, I am not in favour of games or playing as part of a retrospective. The sprint retrospective is a critical opportunity for the team to scrutinise itself and agree on productivity improvements for the next Sprint. The retrospective occurs after the solution review yet before the next Sprint Planning. The Retrospective is a time-boxed, closed-door meeting with a serious purpose – productivity. Typically, the session lasts in hours for the same number of weeks in the sprints. The Scrum Master enables the retrospective and ensures that team members understand the purpose of the retrospective. During this event, the team discusses:

- Their progress or otherwise towards the desired outcome
- The Sprint metrics
- What went well in the Sprint
- What could be improved
- What will they commit to advancing in the next Sprint?

The Scrum Master should encourage the scrum team to be candid to improve its development process and practices to make them more efficient or work more enjoyable for the next Sprint. I have found that these conversations can be focussed by reference to the team's delivery value chain as established during the agile process tailoring activity.

During each Sprint Retrospective, the scrum team identifies ways to increase productivity, efficiency or quality. These improvements may involve revising their delivery process, their documentation and roles and responsibilities. On conclusion of the retrospective, the team should have identified the improvements that it will implement in the next Sprint. These actions should be recorded in a workbook as an audit trail or in case, a review is needed in the future.

Retrospective Ingredients

To have a compelling retrospective, you need several elements. Including:

- Set a place for conducting each retrospective. Ideally, it should be space where the team can discuss without fear of interruption. (In organisations where meeting rooms are at a premium, then booking a place for longer than the anticipated duration will stop the meeting finishing before the retrospective is complete.)

- The whole team should be involved. Scrum recommends gathering all the members together, including the product owners.
- The delivery value chain of the team.
- The team needs candour; establish an open and honest culture in the meeting.
- Ensure all team members not only attend but participate in the meeting, with self-managing comes an obligation for self-improvement.
- Establish a common understanding of how things went between all team members.
- If the team is still learning, then a facilitator who can host the retrospective and ensure participation, this is probably a more significant role than merely the person with a marker pen!
- It is the coach's role to help the team to decide upon the vital few actions that they will take.

The Scrum Master should use a facilitating style, and the outputs are ideas targeted at the improvement of team performance – next sprint! At this step, a team starts a discussion regarding their productivity. Talk with the team about the main issues and find ways to resolve them. It may take time to find the right solutions, formulate and assign tasks.

Recipes for Long-lived Teams

One of the foundational rules of agile is the principle of long-lived teams. This principle stresses that long-lived teams are significant to successfully deriving value from agile practices. The additional benefit is because a long-lived team develops new ways of working and drives their productivity up over time through their continuous improvement activities and retrospectives.

A long-lived team is one comprised of the same individuals which has worked on a problem or product for many months and sometimes even years. They have defined ways of working roles and responsibilities which suit themselves. From a coaching perspective, it is often tempting to leave these teams to self-manage. However, long-lived teams sometimes must change membership and may be seen to have plateaued in terms of productivity.

Long-lived Maintaining a Coaching Position

As a team is long-lived, then they sometimes slip under the coach's radar. It is vital that a coach establishes and maintains a "coaching brief" for these teams. One way may be participation in reviews or retrospectives. It is unlikely that a mature long-lived team will value a teaching style from a coach. However, adopting an "I'm here to learn" approach often delivers the necessary engagement from the team.

Once the coaching position is established, then the coach may use a diagnosis of the metrics or the Agile Health check to encourage performance gains. Often it is in the long-lived teams where systemic challenges become genuinely apparent. Therefore, from a coaching perspective, there is significant value, despite the temptation to do otherwise, to maintain the coaching position.

Avoiding Declining Productivity

As I stated at the outset, agile is about delivering value. If care is not taken at the portfolio level, a long-lived may have declining results in terms of the business value generated over time. The answer is to strengthen the business case such that new features requested from the long-lived team enable the generation of value metrics. By tracking these value metrics, a coach can work with the team to establish viability and continued productivity.

As most will be aware, it is almost impossible to compile inter-team comparisons on velocity, as the basic unit of measure is a variable. However, organisational value delivered over time could be a common denominator where teams can be measured and compared over time.

The Entrées – Serving Suggestions

The recipes provided in this entrée section outline the way that agile is used by single teams. In my view, the fundamental techniques are those relating to risk management and quality assurance. Many of the tools identified use mathematics to identify trends and patterns of team performance.

The entrées include a range of techniques from the world outside of agile, including managing successful programmes and manufacturing cost management. These are tools which an agile coach can use and adapt for their unique coaching context. Many of these techniques will also be applicable for larger teams which are the subject of the next set menu section of this book.

Set Menus – For Programmes and Larger Activities

A Scrum is essentially a one-team, one-sprint at a time thing. So, this begs the question, what if the size of the activity is more work than a Scrum team, that is a team of seven plus or minus two individuals, can deliver in a reasonable timescale? The answer is to scale the team; either by scaling scrum or by aggregating Kanban.

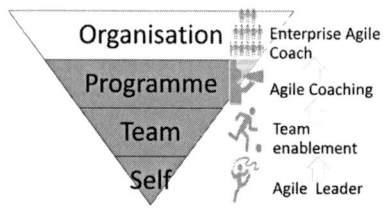

Coaching Layers – Agile Programme Coaching

This set menus section outlines the tools and techniques used by agile coaches, as they work with larger teams or programmes. Coaching in the programme context is like working with individual teams with a few extra multi-team nuances such as all team planning, aligning ways of working and synchronisation.

The skills set used by the agile coach at the programme level build upon those used at the team level. Yet, in their application are used very different from the team level coaching discussed previously. In most situations, larger teams are constructed of several smaller teams. Each smaller team will have a nominated Scrum Master or Kanban Process Manager. The agile coach role, therefore, becomes one of working indirectly with the teams through these smaller team-enabling coaches, but it doesn't preclude direct intervention if the teams request this.

Scaling does not automatically as if by magic, transform an organisation into an agile enterprise. It is merely a means of delivering more significant activities. In this section, I consider the implications from a coaching perspective of moving from an enabler of a single team to the agile coaching of multiple teams – agile programme coaching. In this larger team or programme context, the agile at scale frameworks, such as; LeSS, SAFe, Nexus and Scrum at Scale, all have a part to play.

Working with substantial activities may involve more than one agile coach. Having more than one coach adds complexity to supporting larger teams. Having an agreed set of coaching principles, tools and techniques such as those outlined earlier in the hors d'oeuvre section of the cookbook helps with the consistency and coordination of the coaching approach and interventions.

Working with larger teams and programmes is where Synchrony comes to the fore. For larger teams to operate and use agile principles, they must coordinate and synchronise their activities. The start point is to agree on the standard ways of working and roles and responsibilities in agile process tailoring. For example, the larger team must follow the same delivery life cycle with the same documents, timelines for periodic planning and timely release. They must follow a common iteration or sprint length with agreed integration points. The whole team must understand the clearly defined objectives and solution benchmarks. The entire team must follow the principles of continuous system integration, with the outputs completed by different teams integrated at each sprint to keep the developments in a potentially releasable state. The larger team must establish a common time for internal reviews, system-level QA and customer reviews. Lastly, the team working as a unit should co-ordinate to seek the means of relentless improvement through combined and orchestrated retrospectives.

With larger teams, maintaining individual contribution and motivation may become a challenge. Self-selection is one tool an Agile Coach may use to increase the motivation of team members.

Self-Selecting Teams' Recipe

Self-selection is a facilitated technique for increasing the motivation for team membership. The underlying principle is that organisations get better results when individuals can choose what they work on and with whom they work. Self-selected teams are said to be:

- More productive.
- Increases the understanding that the team is expected to self-organise.
- Have higher degrees of motivation.
- More stable with respect for individual requests to change.
- Happier – with reduced conflict levels.

Self-selection honours the Lean principle of respecting the individual and trusting people with responsibility. It encourages teams to identify and solve complex problems and to organise in a way that's best for the organisation and themselves.

Self-selecting Teams' Ingredients.

Firstly, from the Agile Portfolio Management process provide an outline of all of the activities where team membership is required. What is the solution required, and why is it needed. Most individuals will require more detail than is contained in the initiative brief used in the portfolio prioritisation process. Typical data required is:

- Vision and success criteria.
- The scope and expected activity duration.
- MVP or goals for the next quarter.
- The technical stack.
- Individual talents needed (I.e. specific business or application knowledge, front-end-developer, tester).

Circulate this information freely across the resource pool engaged in the self-selection activity. Also, prepare a summary sheet for each initiative using the initiative name and an outline of the expected talent required.

Assemble the resource pool and allow them to self-assign. Some organisations encourage the product owner to do a sales pitch explaining their initiative and allowing individuals to ask questions. Sometimes rules are needed; occasionally specific preparations are required for individuals who cannot attend in person. Sometimes a form of proportional representation is needed with individuals stating the 1st, 2nd and 3rd choice.

Some organisations have everyone prepare a card, and when making their selection, the individual places their card on the summary sheet. The card should identify the individual's skill set or objectives with joining the team. The facilitator after a short time talks through the summary sheet and the cards attached identifying over-subscribed activities or those still needing talents. If the skills profile is imbalanced, individuals remove their cards from the summary sheets and the process is repeated until all activities have appropriate teams assigned. Some organisations follow the self-selection exercise with a retrospective so that they can learn for the next self-selection workshop.

From a coaching perspective, a self-selecting team session is easy to facilitate providing the line-managers are on board with the self-selecting process or excluded from the event! Having managers deselect team members after the event is something to be avoided!

Large Team Process Tailoring Recipe,

Before big room planning, the teams need to be synchronised, and the agreed agile practices should have a shared understanding across the big team. Agile practices specific to each role will often require training and coaching. It may take between four-to-eight-weeks to ensure everyone understands their role, the ceremonies they will use to ensure collaboration, and what artefacts they will use to plan and execute their part of the overall work. Coaching a big team is an intense and peculiar activity when compared to coaching a single Scrum team.

In an agile process-tailoring workshop, the Agile Coach facilitates the team through several conversations regarding the delivery process. The result of discussions is that the team decides how they're going to work together. The outputs could be simply a table of documents, but I have found that the creation of the team's delivery value chain diagram can be very beneficial. I have used the team's delivery value chain following the large team process tailoring session to clarify decisions and to enable performance improvement conversations during delivery reviews or retrospectives.

Typically, the tailoring conversations are heavily influenced by what the larger team is attempting to achieve. The initial discussion will often be clarification regarding the deliverables and desired outcomes, but it will swiftly move on to conversations about ways of working, roles and responsibilities, the delivery process and the need for documentation.

Again, with the new team, the coach needs to allow time for these discussions, as they are an inherent part of the stages in the Form, Storm, Norm, Perform stages of the Tuckman model[xviii]. With the larger group, these are just as important.

The Big-Room Planning Recipe

According to SAFe big-room, planning usually is two days of planning together with all program and team members every quarter. It is an essential ingredient for more substantial activities. A coordinated planning event brings together all the people in the organisation responsible for delivering the desired solution value. It gives everyone an overview of what everyone else is doing and the understanding of who is dependent on whom and how things are to be coordinated.

Bringing people together this is a literal statement. It's not a figure of speech. The key is to bring them together quite literally, assembling all the stakeholders in the same room in real-time.

Big-room planning represents such a significant commitment by the organisation, but that is in part the point. Planning together to make agile work, requires a commitment across every level of an organisation. While the various scaled agile frameworks provide useful guidelines for the quarterly big room planning, few apart from SAFe, provide comprehensive support. Consequently, while most organisations know how to do sprint planning, many teams struggle with getting one hundred per cent ready for big room planning.

From a coaching perspective, the event needs meticulous planning, preparation and coordination. Big-room planning starts typically with a requirements discovery process. It proceeds through the agile process tailoring. It may involve coordinated value stream mapping, looking at customer feedback, marketing data and the current backlog. The large team takes a high-level pass at the top priority items and the potential key features for the period to be planned. The high-level pass sets us up any actions which are required to understand customer needs, market requirements and the design gaps that need to be addressed before work can be appropriately planned.

The coach's role is one mainly of providing guardrails, organisation, and facilitation. Pre-event meetings are held with product owners to ensure that any significant gaps in understanding are closed before time. Sometimes mentoring is needed for the less experienced product owners, but it is not a time for teaching; unless this is the first such event. Similar meetings happen with the programme level leaders and release train engineers.

Big-room planning preparations make extensive use of checklists, and sometimes teams make use of a Kanban board to plan and control the preparation.

Sometimes, I hear the question, 'Is big-room planning worth it?'

My answer is, 'Two days every quarter is approximately three per cent of people's working time – no matter how many people you have in your program.' So, if big-room planning gives you more than an equivalent of a three per cent gain in productivity, in quality, in delivering value, then time spent in big-room planning is a good investment.

The outcome of the event will be a finalised roadmap, a list of committed features and prioritised stories. A by-product of the event is the alignment of expectations with the stakeholder community and an understanding of the larger team's progression and potential issues.

SAFe calls a big-room planning event PI Planning, but it is very much the same activity. Some teams see the event as an opportunity to take an experimental approach, and the day doesn't have to be perfect. Some teams are comfortable to take away some learnings, and most teams include a retrospective either during the event or after the planning activity.

To Scale a Team or Not?

There is much debate about scaling agile teams; by this, I mean having teams with more members than the Scrum ideal. From an agile coach's perspective, the first question is always, "Why do you want to scale?". Often there is a misconception that scaling means the adoption of agile at the whole organisational level rather than increasing the number of people who are working on the same initiative at the same time. It is true that when some organisations adopt agile, they will need scaling mechanisms for their more substantial teams. Yet not all teams will need these processes.

According to the Scrum Guide,[xix] a single agile team is seven plus or minus two people. The question is, is it necessary to have multiple seven plus or minus two people teams working simultaneously on the same larger initiative from a single backlog? In which case, scaling is relevant. Or will they have multiple teams all working on related, independent activities? (Each team having its own scope definition and product backlog). In which case, scaling is irrelevant.

The problems are entirely different in the first instance the single large team needs organisation and techniques to coordinate and efficiently deliver a large solution. In the second, the organisation needs to introduce Agile Portfolio Management.

Does the organisation believe it needs to scale because they have significantly sized initiatives or because they have lots of developers who need to be kept busy? Or is it because the organisation has announced an "agile transformation" and the immediate thought seems to be that there is a need to "scale" to support that intent.

Often organisations pick an agile framework thinking that it will make them agile – the truth is it probably won't. Scaled agile frameworks provide templates for ways of working with large teams, but each framework has to be tailored to the context, purpose, the culture and the circumstances of the organisation concerned.

While Scrum must be scaled, Kanban does not need scaling in the same way. Kanban teams do not have the same size limitation as Scrum. Yet the flexibility of Kanban has a downside in that it is more difficult to plan using Kanban. Kanban also needs a big upfront planning session, and Kanban is aggregated rather than scaled.

Forecasting using Scrum is also a little more straightforward. A burn-up or burn-down chart gives a clear picture of the expected delivery date. Any variance to plan is immediately observable. Kanban, in contrast, requires complicated calculations using cycle time and Little's Law. Each time, priorities change a repetition of the calculations is required. The recalculation element makes planning with Kanban more difficult and sometimes laborious.

Scaling is Hard

Whatever the reason for scaling, it is recommended to try and avoid scaling to large monolithic teams. Creating great agile Scrum teams is hard work – backbreaking work – scaling them is even more difficult. Scaling increases waste, as it mainly involves the introduction of a coordination or management layer to synchronise and control the outputs of several small teams. Scaling also magnifies any organisational dysfunctions you encounter at the team level.

So, a good rule of thumb as an agile coach is don't consider scaling until you've established good smaller teams. The challenges you will face with scaling include:

- Managing cross-team dependencies. Dependencies are often challenging to track and visualise. Using the product breakdown approach favoured by agile creates a more significant number of dependencies that are created within a single team. Each additional team potentially exponentially increases the number and nature of the dependencies between work items and magnifies the necessity for communication channels between the members of the teams.

- Integration of work often becomes more challenging. Some scaled agile frameworks create a specific integration function; Nexus for example. At some point, certainly, at the end of each iteration, the large team will need to manage the integration of all the work outputs into something that's potentially shippable to the customer.

- Brooks' law. We've known since the mid-nineteen seventies with the Mythical Man-Month[xx] that adding people to a late software project often makes it later. In the same way, merely adding more teams doesn't always ensure that more work gets delivered faster.

- The management of the J-curve effect, or Tuckman's[xxi] stages in group development. Any change made to a people-based process potentially will cause initial productivity decrease (disruption during the Storm period). Then as people get used to the change, hopefully, productivity eventually increases (eventually reaching the perform stage this making the curve monitoring productivity to look like a J). However, the depth and length of the disruption stage are difficult to predict and requires proactive management.

What Can Be Done Instead of Scaling?

There are several things an agile coach should consider to reduce the need for scaling. Things to consider to increase velocity or efficiency of the team before scaling include:

- Is the organisation really, truly agile, or are they using fake agile? Make sure that the teams are not going through the rituals but proactively seeking ways to increase productivity.
- Consider the solution architecture. Can it be redefined in a way which removes the need for teams to work on the same backlog?
- Look at the retrospectives and establish if there are any systemic blockers to increase productivity. See if the retrospectives are useful in seeking ways to increase productivity.
- Has the organisation automated everything it can? Look for handoffs or delays which are created by manual practices.
- Is the work properly organised? Are the backlogs well-prepared? Is the portfolio being well-managed? Can you identify waste?
- Is the team the best it can be? Can they create enough value with a timeline which suits the organisational goals?

The Scaling-Scrum Recipe

To reiterate, scaling Scrum and the scaled agile frameworks are for big teams, not big departments. When the size of a single scrum team limits the development, and more than one scrum team is required, then scaled frameworks are used.

The Scrum of Scrums is a scaling of scrum mechanism. Scrum scales fractally and in doing so, the Scrum of Scrums limits the number of communication pathways needed to transmit information. Scrum of Scrums mirrors the team level daily Scrum except that the Scrum of Scrums is a group composed of representatives from several Scrum teams. The Scrum of Scrum team collaborates to integrate and ship a product(s).

The Scrum Masters and anyone else needed (potentially product owners) collaborate to deliver the large-scale solution. The Scrum of Scrums meets regularly to communicate impediments, progress and any cross-team coordination issues; usually by answering the same three questions used in the Scrum by the smaller teams.

When scaling Scrum, the teams have a single backlog and divide the work items between the individual scrum teams. This forces that activity to have an overarching product owner role who will unless experience require some one-to-one coaching. Having a single backlog means that planning needs coordination. Typically, large teams do this by a big room planning event SAFe uses PI planning LeSS uses a two-stage sprint planning mechanism. The purpose of these planning events is to align teams in terms of cadence, vision and objectives.

With agile at scale, the idea is to have synchronised cadence, sprint cycles, across all the teams. The synchronisation is where all iterations start and end within a day or two of each other. From a coaching, perspective, be aware that all iterations do not necessarily need to complete precisely on the same day. It is acceptable in larger teams to iterations that end over a two or three-day period if they have still applied the principle of continuous integration.

There can be distinct advantages to doing having a very slight offset on the sprint cycles if the offset is not too great. Allowing iterations to end over a two or three-day period can make it easier for someone on multiple teams to attend all the expected to attend review and planning meetings. Additionally, having a slight offset has the advantage of better accommodating team members who may travel into sessions. A distant team member who is on multiple teams will find it easier to justify the travel time and expense if she can participate fully in each of her teams' meetings.

When facilitating a big room planning session, the coach often must remind the teams about project management basics, such as dependencies, risks and time for the integration activities. The coach also when establishing a Scaled Scrum, there are organisational, process and roles and responsibility considerations to be understood.

Aggregating Kanban

Scaling or aggregating Kanban is not a question of team size; it is a question of visualisation and flow. Kanban has scale built-in. So unlike Scrum, you cannot scale Kanban. Using Kanban for more substantial initiatives is merely applying the method to the size of the activity.

Coordination of the inputs and outputs on the relevant boards is required to make the process more efficient. Aggregating Kanban is as the term suggests to the technique of combining elements from various boards to guide a total picture of the activity. Team boards visualise, analyse and control throughput for each team. Summary Boards create management information and control dependencies. In this way, ownership of each board remains with the relevant team, but an overview is also created.

There needs to be some form of cross-team coordination, and so larger Kanban teams have coordination meetings once or twice a week to manage the boundaries between the teams and the control any impediments to efficiency or progress.

The critical factor when scaling Kanban is for the coach to focus on flow rather than for example, the utilisation of individuals.

DevOps Recipes

According to Atlassian, DevOps is a set of practices which automates the process between software development teams building a solution and the IT teams which run the solution. The DevOps practices enable teams to build, test and release software faster and more reliably. It is a broad church and is probably a subject of a book "Coaching DevOps" in its own right!

DevOps is the utopia that everyone has been trying to reach as organisations move from their traditional to more agile ways of working. Some see this as a progressive journey. However, I prefer to see DevOps as an enabler of faster, more regular deliveries if that is what the organisational circumstances demand. There are many standard lists of challenges associated with embedding DevOps in an organisation, and they are typically a mixed bag of people issues, technical constraints and enterprise challenges such as the use of third party or offshore developers. From an agile coaching perspective, every organisation has its unique challenges, and your most significant problem may not even be on the standard list! A common factor, however, is the use of automated testing tools for unit and system testing.

The Agile QA Coach Recipe

Typically, the role of the Agile QA coach is often to help a DevOps team get more mature in the testing area. A team working in a DevOps environment is responsible for the continuous delivery and integration of features. Quality assurance becomes a significant pressure for this team. Agile QA coaching is also applicable to a single team when they wish to automate their testing and deployment activities without fully adopting DevOps. The Agile QA skill set is different and uniquely technical in nature and sits in the area on Technical Mastery in the Agile Coaches Framework referred to earlier.

This coach considers how does this team test their software? What challenges do they face? What should be the balance between manual and automated testing? What is the test coverage in Sprint testing? What were the traps encountered by the team? How many early-life defects were found once the solution was deployed into production?

Agile QA coaching often relates to the implementation of testing and other tools to support agile teams.

The Recipe for Agile Outside of IT

As I outlined earlier, defining agile, a dish of many spices, is complicated. It is even more complicated outside of a technical sphere where the Agile Manifesto; the values and principles are prescriptive around engineering practices. Yet the six elements described earlier in the Hors d'oeuvres are section are as equally relevant to business change activities as they are to software engineering.

Agility in the business sense comes in many different forms depending upon the organisational context. There is general agreement that agility is to do with flexibility, speed of reaction and customer focus. In the broadest sense, these concepts affect strategy, strategic planning, the ability to execute, operations, technology and the innovation processes for products and or services. Agile can be applied to business change with subtle modification.

Agile business change activities should use a backlog. A backlog is a product or solution breakdown structure. Components are linked together in the way that they function or add value. This mapping exercise is as beneficial for business activities, as it is for software activities. The mapping links features associated with a solution with the value they create. During the delivery process, these backlog features are divided into smaller bite-sized work items so that they can be completed by the teams and not inhibit flow.

The concept of collaborative cross-functional teams is easily transferred to business activities. The cross-functional team breaks down the silos of the organisation, many of which inhibit the agile singularity of purpose and speed of delivery. A cross-functional team removes the barriers between organisational silos and provides the efficiency from having different functional experts working together.

All activities, business or software engineering, need to display that they are in control. The essence of agile activity control is visibility combined with mathematical forecasting. The use of metrics is used in planning, controlling and reporting of activity status. With agile activity control, the team meet regularly to establish their status and to communicate with other members of the cross-functional team. These ceremonies will provide robust controls for all types of activities, software or business.

Business teams should adopt the principle of continuous integration. As cross-functional teams reduce the impact of organisational silos, continuous integration minimises the effects of delivery silos. Continuous integration means that work outputs from all of the workstreams are combined so that no one feature or element of the project becomes a silo. In this way, the total solution is regularly evaluated during the delivery process.

Iterative and incremental delivery is a critical aspect of software engineering projects and the same is true with business change activities, perhaps even more so! Some business change activities are extremely difficult if not impossible, to predict and estimate in advance. The agile principles of; horizon and outcome-based planning, coupled with referential estimating, work exceptionally well in unpredictable business circumstances. The adaptive approach of PDCA testing concepts and learning fits well in some business circumstances. Developing a plan and set of requirements for the early stages and then returning to refine designs several times based upon customer feedback is more productive and faster in the longer term.

Agile Outside of IT Ingredients

From a coaching perspective, there is little to choose between a software engineering team and a business change team except for the personalities involved. Business Change activities tend to have a greater mixture of job-grades or perceived seniority. Depending upon organisational culture, this may present the coach with additional challenges with the daily stand-ups and coordination activities.

At the beginning of a business change activity, it may be necessary for the coach to spend time with all parties to ensure that they all fully understand the agile principles and ceremonies. Agile process tailoring will need to be undertaken with care, as the team may need to "find" the appropriate artefacts and ceremonies.

The backlog will almost certainly need to include; stakeholder management activities, change management actions, benefits realisation tasks in addition to the development activities.

Set Menus – Serving Suggestions

Agile at scale is about equipping larger teams to deliver with agility. It is not necessarily about enterprise agility. The emphasis with larger teams is synchronisation. The iteration plans, delivery mechanisms and the means of assuring quality need coordination and to be synchronised. The principles of continuous integration need to be applied. Roles and responsibilities at the Scrum team and at the more substantial team, levels need to be established and staffed.

Transformational Dinner Parties!

A dinner party is where all the recipes selected by the chief are served up to the guests. Planning and executing an agile transformation is similar. An agile transformation is where it all comes together from a coaching perspective, the self-organisation skills, the ability to support teams and larger teams or programmes and change management practices are combined to improve the organisation.

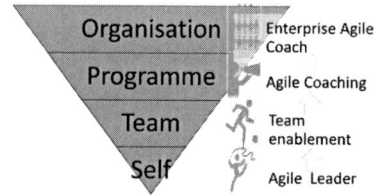

Coaching layers – the Enterprise Agile Coach

At this level, the Enterprise Agile Coach or consultant builds on the agile coaching and team enablement skills identified earlier but, now requires finely-tuned change management techniques.

Enterprise Agile Coaching focuses primarily on people, the organisation, how they work together and how they relate to each other. It's not just developing a framework or introducing new methods and tools. It is about facilitating better processes; how the organisation gets things done. It is about the structural and cultural change to increase agility and fulfil strategic plans.

The recipes in this section are primarily for agile transformations. These recipes concentrate on optimising the whole of the delivery value chain rather than a single team or programme component of it. These recipes can result in new business agility for the organisation concerned. They use those Technical,

111

Business and Transformational Mastery areas referenced in the Agile Coaching Framework.

Leading an agile transformation is a significant responsibility for an Enterprise Agile Coach. As when organising a dinner party at home, there are many considerations; the guests, the menu, the elements of the party. Leading an agile transformation is very similar; it is about understanding the organisational objectives, the awareness of the stakeholder's personalities, the pressure for change and then making the necessary changes happen.

Often, the plan for a transformation prepared by a coach is thwarted by ingrained organisational behaviours and resistance to change. In this section, I look at the critical recipes for working through resistance to a successful transformation.

I take lessons from the "sharp-end" of agile transformation; as an Agile Coach or consultant pursuing the means to purposefully changing an organisation.

Such change needs cautious preparation, execution and management. As in most organisations, these changes happen while teams continue to deliver products and services to customers. Risks must, therefore, be appropriately assessed, and operational capabilities preserved during transformation.

Many organisations embark upon the "agile transformational journey" only to find that what looked relatively simple in planning, is far more complicated in reality. The complexity is in the degree and magnitude of the change and the fact that there is no one prescribed solution which works for all organisation.

Despite what many "branded" consultancies advertise, there really is no set pattern to success for senior executives to follow. As the DNA of each organisation is unique, the reasons for market success and the strategic vision are distinctive, so the means to alter these formulae must also be inimitable.

Much of the wisdom, the books, academic papers, webcasts and videos, concerning agile, are focused at the team level. The agile transformation about the combination and adoption of these agile team principles at the business or organisational level. It is as much about behaviour and organisational change as it is about Scrum or Kanban! It, therefore, presents senior leaders with challenges which they need to work out for themselves without such recommendations. The temptation is to reach out to their traditional business advisors; however, this may not be an optimal approach.

I have found two models useful to assist the work of the Enterprise Agile Coach. The first is a process model for the Enterprise Coaching. The second is a model which explains the stages of an agile transformation.

Enterprise Agile Coaching Recipe

I have found a four-stage transformation model as a useful reference. The four stages are Analysis – where the reasons for adopting agile are established and the targeted improvements defined. Tailoring – where the coach works with stakeholders to define the agile methodology and ecosystem. Delivery – where the changes are rolled out in a planned systemic way. Adapt – the final stage in the PDCA cycle, where inspect and adapt logic is applied to the organisational change process itself.

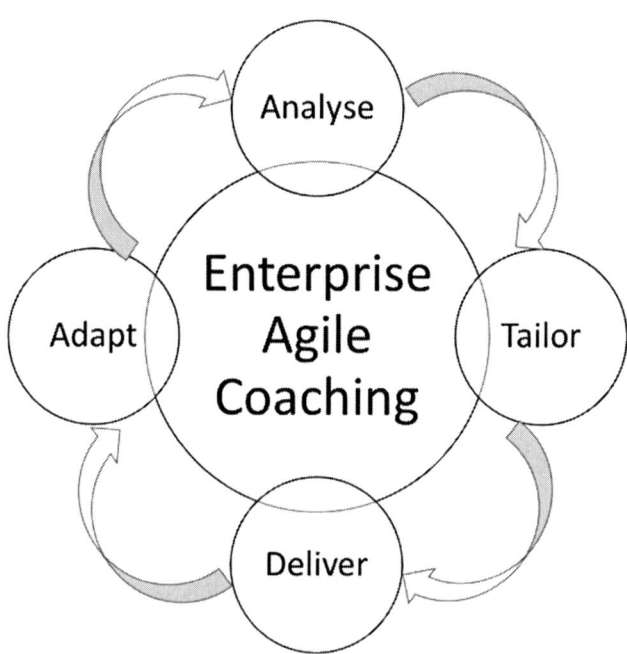

Enterprise Agile Coaching Model

Enterprise agile coaching is always contextual and therefore requires the coach to undertake a situational analysis to fully understand the strategic challenges and the rationale for adopting agile. This analysis stage is foundational, and while not lengthy, rigour is required.

113

In many market sectors, the journey to becoming more agile is a strategic imperative. Yet despite this pressure, for many reasons, some organisations find this transition extremely difficult. The challenges encountered point to the existing practices, processes and cultures as the source of potential hurdles. As the DNA of each organisation is unique in this regard, each will need to develop a unique map of the journey toward its agile goal. This transition map needs to address culture, process and capability improvements as a way of altering this organisational DNA.

Identifying and tailoring the appropriate agile techniques and processes is a fundamental Enterprise Agile Coaching skill. To function organisations, need more than team level improvements. They need mechanisms for funding, resourcing and monitoring the agile activities. They need means of ensuring product quality and processes for deploying solutions to customers. The implementation of agile at the organisational level nearly always involves the creation or introduction of a lightweight agile methodology. This methodology establishes the mechanisms for starting, monitoring and governing the agile activities. The method is usually based upon one or more of the agile-at-scale frameworks or Kanban, but may also embed some elements from traditional waterfall frameworks such as Managing Successful Programmes[xxii].

The Deliver element involves organisational change management skills on the part of the coach. In that, the coach considers the end-to-end value chain, establishes what needs to change then makes the change happen. It is more than merely working with teams; it is the organisational consideration of how people, the leadership and management need to change to transition to new ways of working. Often the transformation involves substantial process re-engineering and the introduction of modern tooling or technical elements.

The Adapt element is an essential part of the framework completing the PDCA cycle. This element allows the coach to "pilot" new ways of working to establish revised working practices. Without the Adapt element, processes must be polished and finalised and organisational changes implemented. Having the Adapt element allows prototyping, modification and refinement as the organisation changes.

Why is Agile so Hard? The Situational Analysis

The first stage of the model, the situational analysis encourages the Enterprise Agile Coach to consider traditional organisational behaviours and practices.

When some say "why is becoming agile so hard", it is because an organisation is forced to confront its poor operational practices, and its management behaviours to increase agility. These are the essential ingredients of organisational DNA and are the core means by which the organisation was previously operating. Analysing how the existing processes and behaviours enforce the corporate culture is, therefore, an essential step in the understanding of the Enterprise Agile Coach and allows them to establish what must change.

When analysed objectively, organisational practices have grown up over time. Often these were implemented to solve problems now long gone. Many of these processes in a project context, add cost, formalise delays, create bureaucracy and blur the lines of responsibility and control. Some existing working practices – not at the team but the enterprise level – are often primary impediments to an organisation becoming more agile and therefore need to be identified and understood.

The Agile Manifesto and the agile principles, when applied at the enterprise level, often defy much of the established organisational wisdom. The mere act of an Enterprise Agile Coach proposing changes to these foundations, even though accepted necessity at the intellectual level, often provokes emotional reactions in the middle to senior management layers which the coach must counter. These reactions make the adoption of agile operationally extremely difficult to digest.

Agile makes individuals and teams accountable and encourages the interaction of people over rigid processes. Agile practices focus on value delivery in the shortest lead-time. Agile introduces ceremonies and perceived "process" shortcuts. The absence of documentation and the devolution of responsibilities away from middle management also causes managerial alarm. With jobs or roles threatened, resistance to adopting the necessary changes often escalates.

From a coaching perspective, this means it is essential to have clarity of what needs to change and is the reason why the situational analysis activity is so crucial.

Sharing observations and recommendations with key stakeholders encourages understanding of how their organisation needs to change and the reasons why. Often senior and middle management require data to accept the need for change. There is an onus on the Enterprise Agile Coach to identify benchmark data, before the change and to collect the same data as KPIs following the change so that the beneficial impacts can be established.

Relating the potential improvements from implementing agile to the strategic organisational goals, creates a dialogue which encourages collaboration and involvement. Using data often turns the experience into a dispassionate conversation for the Enterprise Agile Coach.

Agile introduces new roles and responsibilities. It also breaks the boundaries, the them-and-us culture, which may have evolved in some firms between business functions. The concepts of collaboration and one-team may require some enterprises to embark upon organisational "healing" efforts; building trust between business functions where animosity previously existed. In this case, the Enterprise Agile Coach will need to create opportunities for building trust and establishing new working relationships which are more than simply deploying a Scrum Team!

Systemic "Blockers" Recipe

The key to a successful agile implementation is not just the training or the upskilling of people, although these are essential aspects, it is identifying ways to systematically overcome the structural, procedural and cultural barriers that are obstructing organisational performance improvement.

In Scrum, anything that stops the delivery of a product, or acts as a hurdle for the team is termed an impediment or blocker. An impediment is an obstacle which prevents progress. It could be an issue or bug discovered during development or testing and which does not allow progress. When working with larger teams, blockers may occur, which impact one or more delivery teams. The larger the number of teams blocked, the more serious is the problem encountered. An impediment doesn't necessarily have to be a complete showstopper; instead, it could have the effect of slowing the activity down. Sometimes, a blocker may be systemic and impact all or several large and small teams. These are the impediments which are of concern in the case of an agile transformation.

Removing these ecosystem type impediments requires executive support, money and time. For resolution, engagement is often needed from one or more senior executives, middle managers and sometimes from other agile teams. Short sprint cycles and delivery lead times put pressure on the speed of executive decision-making and issue resolution. In many occasions, systemic and large-scale blockers need additional managerial muscle for resolution, with the result that the Enterprise Agile Coach may need to call upon the services of an Executive Action Team.

Executive Action Team Recipe

To truly reap the benefits of agile, the C-Suite or senior leaders must lead the cultural change. How? By firstly having clarity regarding why the organisation is implementing agile and then to operate as an Executive Action Team (EAT) who form and swarm to resolve the problems encountered.

An EAT is a small cross-functional team suggested by Scrum@Scale; executives who understand how the agile ceremonies, roles and tools work together to enable the expected increase in productivity. The EAT members collaborate to remove the organisational or systemic blockers. The EAT is not a steering group, far from it, it facilitates the agile change by innovation and problem-solving. Taking these actions often involves the individuals' in the emotional aspects of cultural change leadership and requires them to learn and communicate their learnings to the rest of the enterprise.

Executive Action Team Ingredients

To be effective, an EAT needs to have the organisation credibility and influence to be able to resolve the specific impediment encountered. It is therefore unlikely that forming a single EAT to solve every problem encountered in a transformation will be useful. It would have potentially too many senior executives so to be unwieldy. The Enterprise Agile Coach should seek an EAT formed explicitly to resolve an impediment. The EAT would be made up of senior individuals who have the organisation responsibilities or remit to make effective changes. The role of the Enterprise Agile Coach would be to initiate each EAT and ensure that they have enough data to know why a change is needed.

In some instances, due to timescales, the EAT may define a quick fix to resolve the immediate problem encountered by a team and then do a second fix to permanently resolve the challenge and clear the way for all teams. In making the change, they also define the means to measure whether their resolution is sufficient. The check activity comes next where the EAT collects data ensuring that they have the desired results. In this way, the EAT is a typical usage of the Deming PDCA Cycle. If there are still issues, then the EAT adjusts the original fix to resolve the challenge. Typically, the agile coach is involved in the Plan and Adjust activities but leaves the EAT to make the changes and perform the measures.

Lean-Agile PMO as a Catalyst

When an organisation chooses to adopt agile ways of working, they often first turn to the PMO as the owner of the project ecosystem and an agile coach could be wise to do the same thing. A PMO typically understands the portfolio risks, the individuals, the organisational constraints, the critical success criteria for each initiative. The PMO, therefore, has a wealth of knowledge which an experienced coach can make use of to accelerate the pace of agile adoption. Sometimes agile coaches think the PMO is going to be a defunct organisation once an agile transformation is complete. I have experienced the opposite situation where because of the new ways of working senior management increase their reliance on the PMO requiring assurance that an activity is being managed within the organisation's risk parameters.

Where the coach is considering the introduction of continuous integration and continuous deployment (CICD) or DevOps, the switch from project orientation and cost to a process flow delivery approach has significant consequences for the PMO function. Again, the PMO needs to be involved and its processes altered so that CICD may be used and the organisational requirements for information met through the auspices of the PMO.

In many mature organisations, the PMO also has a portfolio management responsibility deciding or recommending which activities are started and when. Portfolio management deals with how an organisation identifies, prioritises, organises and manages different activities. Portfolio Management seeks to optimise the value created for the organisation in the long run. Agile through its incremental delivery approach and its alternative ways of prioritising activities based on the cost of delay rather than return on investment as presents a need for significant change within the PMO.

PMO As a Catalyst Ingredient

I have started several agile adoption activities with training the PMO. Often there are many misconceptions regarding agile across an organisation enlisting the PMO to dispel some of these misapprehensions frees time for the Enterprise Agile Coach.

As the PMO owns the delivery ecosystem, they also need to know and understand the impact and principles of agile in their organisation. Having the PMO prepared and able to communicate the transformational journey is a massive asset to an agile adoption activity.

The PMO may need to adjust itself progressively as the transformation advances, for example, as more teams adopt agile techniques or when there is a need to start to use Agile Portfolio Management. For these incremental adjustments, I use a workshop and continue with the value chain mapping approach described earlier.

Value stream mapping is a powerful technique. If organisational agility is the goal, it is as well to start as far back as the idea formulation stage as often some aspects of solution delivery are "cast in stone" at a very early stage. PMO involvement usually starts early on with the operation of the portfolio and investment management processes.

Some frameworks, such as SAFe, suggest establishing a Lean-Agile Centre of Excellence (LACE). The responsibilities identified by SAFe are to facilitate agile adoption through training, coaching and the provision of guidance regarding tools and techniques. In my experience, if a PMO is a centre of excellence for organisational solution delivery having a separate function, a LACE in addition to a PMO is unnecessary. In my experience, once an organisation is in business-as-usual mode, that is post-transformation, the PMO is the natural organisational home for agile coaches.

Agile Portfolio Management Recipe

When managing the portfolio, the Lean-Agile PMO needs to be confident in the agile process, but also accept that some projects may be using a waterfall approach with others using continuous delivery. Portfolio Management in the agile world has some similarities with traditional portfolio processes. For example, initiative prioritisation is undertaken using a Risk-Value approach. However, with agile, the PMO needs to be able to respond to incremental delivery and accept the absence of detailed definitions of scope and make use of the Agile Release Schedule and Minimum Viable Product definition.

Agile Portfolio Management allows organisations to identify, prioritise and execute initiatives or parts of initiatives which optimise the strategic gain. It gives clarity when activities will not deliver the anticipated benefits or when further investment in a product or activities will no longer provide the desired outcomes. Analytics are used to identify potential investments with falling returns or unfunded activities which can present a more significant strategic gain than some in-flight activities. Agile Portfolio Management is, therefore, as much about stopping or reprioritising activities as it is about starting them.

Typically, organisations have three competing inputs drivers for investment. The first source of input is strategic initiatives. During strategic planning, the organisation evaluates options and determines the need for action. These actions create initiatives which are sub-divided into prioritised and actionable agile work items. The second source is market requirements, regulatory changes, responding to competitor's actions and so on generate a second group of activities. Market requirements often have fixed dates and fixed scope definitions for the organisation to achieve compliance. The final source of work is the myriad of small changes needed for efficiency or productivity improvement under the banner of continuous improvement.

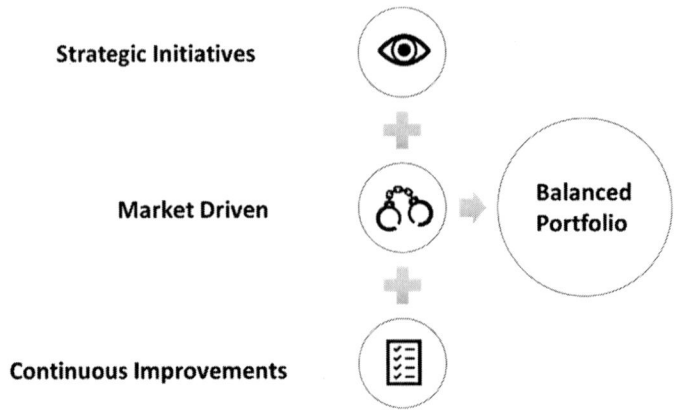

Strategic Initiatives

Market Driven

Balanced Portfolio

Continuous Improvements

Creating a balance portfolio

In an ideal world, a portfolio plan should provide a line of sight from the creation of the vision to the achievement of the strategic aim. However, this is rarely the case. Organisational priorities change. The anticipated benefits from plans set out months, sometimes years in advance may be reduced by changing market conditions or competitor activity. Assumptions made at the time of the business case creation may be subsequently found to be invalid. Organisations in volatile markets will need to validate and revise their portfolio plans more often than those in more stable environments. The consequence is that portfolio management is an on-going process which includes the monitoring of benefits realised.

Portfolio Management Recipes

Agile Portfolio Management emphasises organisational value delivered. It focuses on investment decisions on the activities that produce the highest return. It continuously encourages those making investment decisions and the teams delivering, to continually consider the viability of the iterative activity.

Agile Portfolio Management significantly alters the approach to the allocation of resources; money, time and people. The Enterprise Agile Coach will need actions to build executive trust in the new methods. Agile is not anarchy and, in many ways, has much stronger process elements than many traditional approaches. For example, in numerous organisations, the linkage between the strategic plans and strategy execution is weak. Due to the agile emphasis on value created, I have found that agile improve the contents of the business case regarding measurable benefits. I have also found that as the agile teams retain awareness of the business case throughout the delivery process; ensuring that the targeted benefits are really delivered.

Regularly checking the viability of each investment encourages teams to maximise and clearly illustrate the organisational value delivered or anticipated. In doing this, it strengthens the link between the work undertaken and the strategic plans. It is this continual verification of the change investment portfolio that provides the organisational agility; the ability to start activities and to stop them if another initiative appears which has a greater benefit or more significant strategic priority.

Rolling Wave Portfolio Planning Ingredients

The basic idea with rolling wave portfolio planning is that you plan things that are closer in time to now in detail and things that are distant in time at a summary or higher level. The logic is that the further away in time that an activity is planned, the higher the chance that it will change during that time; therefore, any investment in thinking through the details is likely wasted. You still want to plan at a high level to guide your current decisions and to set stakeholder's expectations as to what is likely to occur in the future, but putting placeholders in time is the limit of the planning.

True agile delivery practices give more opportunity to close out delivery activities than many traditional approaches. As one investment banker told me recently, 'This organisation is great at kicking off projects but very bad at stopping them.'

In rolling wave planning, the organisation continually checks that it is maximising the opportunity from its strategic investments. Yet it also seeks to limit the amount of work in progress at any one time, so that flow and throughput are maximised. Rolling wave planning may make use of a portfolio Kanban. In which case, the Kanban shows a prioritised backlog, the activities that are in-flight and those activities which are completed and delivering results.

Benefits management processes would suggest that collecting the benefits realised data would help the organisation make better investment decisions and ensure that the focus remains on the organisational value delivered.

Agile Transformation Stages Recipe

The second model I find useful describes the sequence of stages in an agile transformation. This model makes the elements Tailor, Deliver and Adapt from the Enterprise Agile Coaching model explicit.

While there is no set pattern followed by all organisations, the adoption of agile typically goes through three generic stages:

1. Exploration.
2. Formalisation.
3. Normalisation.

I find senior executives relate to these three stages and understand that the Formalisation step is where the transformation takes place. Consequently, Formalisation is more complicated than the other stages.

Exploration, as the name suggests, is when small teams within an organisation use agile techniques and are deemed to be successful. The exploration stage is characterised by teams experimenting, using different approaches based upon their interpretation of agile.

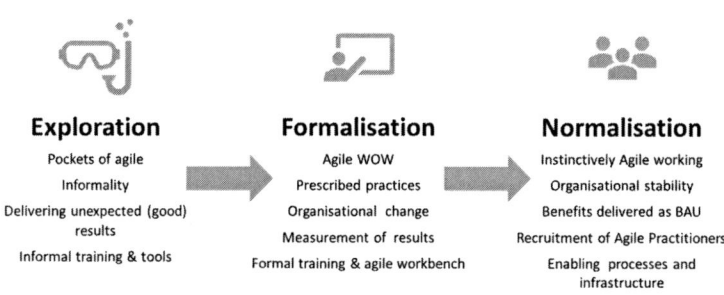

Exploration	**Formalisation**	**Normalisation**
Pockets of agile	Agile WOW	Instinctively Agile working
Informality	Prescribed practices	Organisational stability
Delivering unexpected (good) results	Organisational change	Benefits delivered as BAU
Informal training & tools	Measurement of results	Recruitment of Agile Practitioners
	Formal training & agile workbench	Enabling processes and infrastructure

Agile Transformation Stages

These experimenting teams deliver results which in some way, challenge the organisational norms. Senior leadership then decides that based upon these small successes, they wish to take agile to the next stage. That is to formally adopt agile working practices across the entire organisation or within specific operations.

The Formalisation stage is the actual agile transformation itself and is therefore quite complicated. Success in the Formalisation stage is mostly a question of senior leadership resolve, coupled with the coach's expertise. Senior leaders will find the necessity to accept adjustments to some of the organisational rituals or traditions to achieve the change in capability. The coaches require clarity of purpose, knowledge of a range of agile techniques, change management skills and tenacity!

Formalisation is characterised by the creation of the agile ways of working and enabling the teams to use and adapt these practices. It also involves the introduction of lightweight standards appropriate for the organisation. These standards harmonise some of the techniques which were useful in the experimenting team and make them organisationally applicable.

Formalisation also involves the organisational changes needed to make the agile teams efficient, portfolio management and PMO governance. It is also where the agile coach benchmarks performance and starts to measure the improvements made. Mobilising teams involves training but also frequently consists of the introduction of a new workbench of tools to support agile activities. It is traditionally this formalisation step which is generically referred to as the agile transformation.

The formalisation stage is complicated, and it is often a long journey and therefore requires planning. In creating the transformation plan there is a necessity to anticipate the incremental elements and sequence of change, to predict the likely outcomes, and prepare where possible, a reaction should adaptation of the plan be required. In formalisation change is needed at three levels,

1. Changing the behaviour of teams. In normal circumstances, this is a relatively straightforward adaptation; introducing new roles, new processes and control frameworks. With training, coaching and middle management support, the transition takes time and message repetition, nevertheless changing the behaviour of teams is not such a significant challenge compared to altering the functioning of the organisation.

2. Altering the primary functional drivers of behaviour. These primary behavioural drivers are typically the operational functions which may feel threatened by the formalisation of agile. They, therefore, need careful management and a focus on the transformation. These functions often include; the PMO, Procurement, Finance (some aspects of the financial governance), Resource Management (i.e. how peoples time is planned and Human Resources. These functions have classically embedded processes, measures and controls which enforce results by behavioural or process means. These mechanisms need to be identified, disabled or replaced, by methods which align with the agile goals.

3. Changing the measures and metrics. There is a need to realign all the business metrics. As business metrics provide controls or indicators, they establish and enforce the organisational behavioural norms. Many of these measures, used at the corporate or individual level, will need revision, so they re-enforce and encourage the desired agile behaviours, rather than providing a source of contradiction.

Many successful transformations use internal agile champions or ambassadors in conjunction with the Enterprise Agile Coaches. The agile champions are individuals, from different parts (and levels) of the organisation, which have internal credibility and typically have business operations expertise. These champions are mobilised with a passion about the transformational potential of agile and due to their specialist knowledge are used to assist the organisational transition.

The agile champions undertake actions in the transformational plan and attempt to remove as many organisational impediments to reaching the new capability as is needed. The Enterprise Agile Coach works closely with the champions as an external catalyst.

Normalisation is when agile behaviours become second nature to the people and are the natural choice for new activities and business as usual. It is:

- When the organisation is consistently choosing to work using agile.
- When all the agile related organisational changes are complete.
- The need to monitor the agile benefits generated have been replaced by business-as-usual KPIs.

Some say that an agile transformation is never complete, and I understand this view. However, my contention is if an agile mindset and agile delivery are commonplace, and the organisation has taken relentless improvement seriously, and the strategy is driving Agile Portfolio Management then the transformation is complete.

Exploration – The Initial Stage

Exploration is the stage leading up to the "let's do agile" decision – the tipping point from where transformation takes over.

The tipping point is typically reached when three factors are aligned:

1. When there is a strategic imperative to adopt new ways of working or when c-suite executives have seen the results of the experimentation in agile and wish to expand these effects to the whole organisation.
2. When leadership is committed to investing their time and effort in proactively sponsoring the necessary change.

3. That there is an appetite to invest and sustain the investment to allow the level organisational development needed.

The definition of business agility is about the organisation's ability to adapt, change quickly and renew in a volatile market environment. It is also about the capacity to adjust strategy and test the results as they go rapidly. It is about altering the organisation, adapting or inventing new processes and for some the absorption of modern technology.

Yet many senior executives deciding to "let's do agile" do not understand the full ramifications of this pronouncement! It also may be true that immediately after they draw this conclusion is not the most appropriate time politically for the agile coach to explain! (Often this is better left to the transformation planning stage when these sponsors can be involved in choices regarding the paths and approaches to reach their objectives.)

The exploratory initiatives are often characterised by not waiting for top management approval; they have just happened. Some may have begun their journey as a result of customers or suppliers. Acting without central authority or budget resources, they have scored early successes. These skunkworks type activities have limited ability to acquire the organisational knowledge, broad leadership support or the social capital to make a significant structural or administrative change. Consequently, these agile initiatives limited to small parts of an organisation, tend to quickly run into conflicts with the traditional roles in the organisation who are attempting to preserve the status quo.

When leading a transformation, these pockets of agile may present an opportunity for the Enterprise Agile Coach if these teams are genuinely using agile. Alternatively, they may also offer a challenge if they are "agile in name only". They may also assist with the identification of potential anti-agile managerial patterns and sadly, they may also power resistance to change in some instances. Consequently, some of these initiatives may require reshaping in the future to align with the organisational way of doing agile.

Not everyone uses agile in the way outlined in the SAFe literature, the Scrum Guide or indeed as described earlier in this cookbook. Some people use the term agile to refer to any team, breaking the norms, stepping away from governance standards, calling itself, or simply claiming to be, agile. This usage leads to many teams which might be called "agile in name only" or what is referred to as "fake agile".

In other words, to understand whether a team is genuinely Agile, a coach must look at the way those teams are operating. They may be using the ceremonies and processes of "Agile" but without the metrics, the Agile mindset or agile quality assurance. Scott Ambler[xxiii] suggested the following five criteria to determine if a team is truly agile:

1. Working software – agile teams produce working software regularly, typically in the context of short, stable, time-boxed iterations.
2. Active stakeholder participation – agile teams work closely with their stakeholders, ideally daily.
3. Regression testing – agile teams do, at a minimum, continuous developer regression testing. Disciplined agile teams take a Test-Driven Development (TDD) approach.
4. Organisation – agile teams are self-organising, and disciplined agile teams work within an appropriate governance framework at a sustainable pace. Agile teams are also cross-functional "whole teams", with enough people with the proper skills to address the goals of the team.
5. Improvement – Agile teams regularly reflect on, and disciplined teams also measure how they work together and then act to improve on their findings promptly[1].

Again, the Exploration stage may not be the time to draw senior management attention to such deficiencies in the experimenting teams. Particularly, if the data from these teams were the basis for their "go-agile" decision, the need for a little "correction" by the coach may be better left to the formalisations stage when the new ways of working have been fully defined and these in-flight agile working practices can be adjusted if necessary.

An essential use of these experimenting teams is to collect some metrics for future comparison purposes. These teams provide an in-organisational benchmark of potential improvement, which often has far more relevance for senior executives than external data. These benchmark metrics can be used by the coach in the future during the transformation to illustrate the benefits which the new ways of working have brought to the organisation.

---

[1] (This paper was written before Scott Ambler created the Disciplined Agile framework.)

Essential Benchmarks Recipe

As a principle, agile teams concentrate on outcomes rather than outputs. The same is true of teams of agile coaches. Measuring the results is an essential element of transformation. Creating benchmarks and establishing measurable improvement goals are, therefore, a necessary part of the agile coach's toolkit.

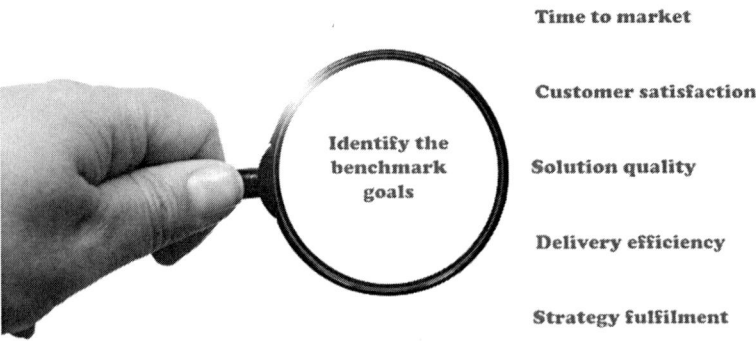

Essential benchmarks

Success for an agile coach will be the demonstrable achievement of the desired outcomes. Care should be taken that the desired outcomes are within the team and the coach's sphere of influence. However, sometimes establishing the benchmarks means creating new sets of management information with its associated validation and lack of certainty. Typically, most organisations will require more than a team maturity assessment. They will expect outcomes which align to their business objectives or strategy.

Benchmark data, therefore, needs to be established at the outset of the transformation, and these metrics should be monitored on an ongoing basis by the coaching team. At any point, coaches should have the information to hand to enable them to answer the question "what have we achieved?" immediately!

We Tried It Once but...

All organisations have past "flavour of the month" initiatives in their history. Traditionally, these initiatives are described with a phrase starting something like this. "We tried XYZ once, but... This preface is always followed by an organisational tale of woe together with the speaker's analysis why something didn't succeed.

Failure of the flavour of the month scenario could be the result of poor execution, or changes in priorities of executives, or the replacement of a senior leader, or the initiative has been allowed to fade because the apparent driver has disappeared.

The coach should link the adoption of agile to the organisational strategic imperatives. Using the benchmark data, the measurable improvements and the successes achieved to illustrate progression towards the transformational goals. These actions will prevent this erosion of purpose even when sponsorship changes. In later sections of this book, I will outline how these, and other tasks help coaches achieve beneficial agile.

Formalisation – the Transformation Stage

Agile transformations as organisational and cultural change initiatives cannot merely be planned out on a Gant chart; in fact, the transformation itself is an ideal candidate for an agile plan and control approach.

People and organisations are not machines where pulling a lever results in a change of gear! So, a command-and-control approach with a meticulous list of activities is unlikely to succeed. Yet some structure is required, and, in this section, I will offer suggestions for the contents and construction of this plan.

The agile transformation organisational change plan is incredibly adaptive in nature. Planned activities may not have the desired effect in terms of increased capability or changes in behaviour. Transformational plans are a prime example of the use of the Plan, Do, Check, Act, Deming[xxiv] or Shewhart cycle. This technique allows for the adaptation which cultural change requires. It uses the Check and Act elements to provide transformational control.

The critical skills used by the Enterprise Agile Coach in leading a transformation are the Technical, Business and Transformational Mastery areas of the Agile Coaching Framework together with a detailed knowledge of change management coupled with personal behavioural skills. Namely, these personal traits are:

- Personal resilience or the ability to stay focussed when challenged or politically thwarted.
- A capacity to generate trust.
- Talent to build a network of mutually supporting individuals.
- An aptitude to train, coach and mentor at all organisational levels.
- The gift to simplify and develop clarity.
- Capability to help others manage uncertainty.
- Organised, the ability to: plan, control and adjust activities based upon the situations encountered.
- Talent to follow through remembering the detail commitments to individuals and teams.

I have found that these skills of the Enterprise Agile Coach need to be applied in a way which builds senior executive's confidence in the coach and the transformation process.

To provide a checklist and assist with the construction of the plan, I use a nine-step transformation process and my initial starting point.

Step 1 – The Formal "Go-Agile" Decision

Step 1. Is the decision by senior management to formally adopt agile as a means of operating part or the whole of the business?

At the "go-agile" decision point, senior executives face a crucial choice. Do they wish to limit the use of agile and its benefits; efficiency of delivery, speed, customer focus and employee satisfaction to certain areas? Or do they wish to potentially unlock higher value by changing the entire operating model so that agile becomes the organisational norm, rather than an alternative?

Committing to an entirely new operating model requires careful consideration and a transformational approach, led from the top. The Enterprise Agile Coach requires finely polished change management skills irrespective of the nature or size of the transformation.

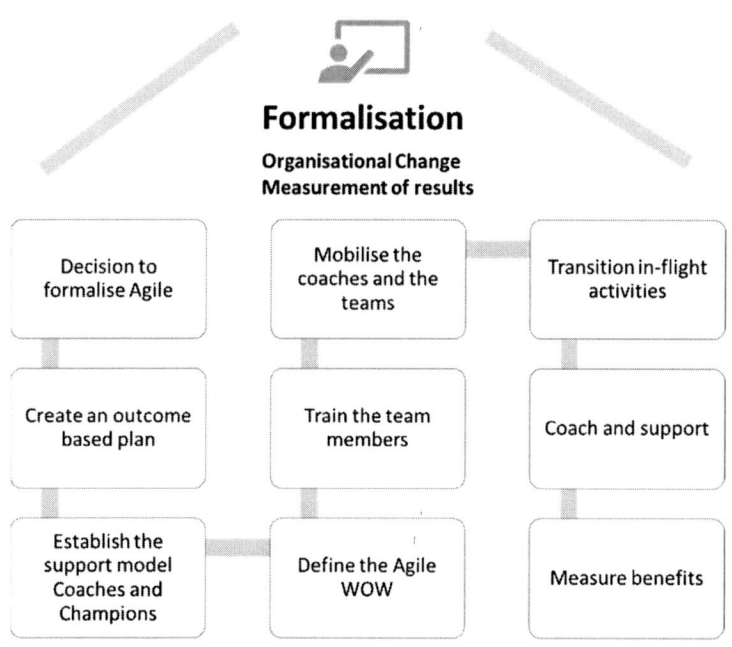

Formalisation
Organisational Change
Measurement of results

Decision to formalise Agile	Mobilise the coaches and the teams	Transition in-flight activities
Create an outcome based plan	Train the team members	Coach and support
Establish the support model Coaches and Champions	Define the Agile WOW	Measure benefits

Nine step transformation process

The Why Agile? Recipe – The Link Between Strategy and Agile

The coach needs to thoroughly understand the organisation driver to become agile. Unless it is a project business, being agile is rarely the organisational driver for a change as disruptive and all-encompassing as an agile transformation. It is usual for an organisation to decide it needs to be more agile because of a strategic reason.

Many organisations, challenged by new market entrants, tech companies and blurred industry lines, are looking to drive sustained growth and unique competitive advantage and they seek to respond by increasing agility. The organisation consequently pursues business agility by embarking in agile, digitisation and technology innovation initiatives.

An agile transformation can take place on a large or small scale; it can involve the front, middle or back-office; it can be conducted by any enterprise, from a start-up to global unicorn agile transformation, it will affect many aspects of the organisation's structure, including such functions as innovation, finance, marketing, sales, human resources and operations.

Business agility is the ability of an organisation to identify changes internally or externally and swiftly respond to continue to deliver its value to its customers. Business agility is related to not a specific methodology or even a framework. Instead, it is an organisational frame of mind combined with an operating model.

An Enterprise Agile Coach needs to fully understand why the organisation is introducing agile before deciding on what type of agile to employ. I have earlier outlined the use of the Agile Coaching Triangle even when working at the Enterprise level; these principles still apply and impact the ways that the coaches operate. This contextual understanding also allows the coach to define appropriate measures for success – the desired outcomes for their time invested in transformational activities.

An agile transformation will test the determination of the senior leadership in an organisation. Agile adoption is a complex activity which saps organisational time, energy and effort. The change, therefore, needs clear and distinct objectives to succeed. I have found the following checklist useful when defining an agile transformation and taking the actions to make the new agile ways of working "stick". To be successful, the transformation needs:

- A compelling reason why building agile capabilities is necessary for strategic objectives or specific intent,
- A plan which describes the establishment of those capabilities, outcomes, within time as horizon goals.
- Recognition by senior leaders that the plan will need to be adaptive. Reacting to the resistance which organisational change often encounters.
- Clarity over the appropriate use of external expertise. Using such capabilities as a catalyst and using internal agile champions as the vital change agents.
- That monitoring and measuring progress towards the establishment of the strategic capabilities is essential.

Transformation Business Case Recipe

The typical response to changes in market situations is a transformation initiative – a top-down restructuring, accompanied by across-the-board cost-cutting, a technological reboot and some agile reengineering. Such a significant endeavour will require investment, and therefore most organisations will need a business case to be prepared. Typically, a business case will require an explanation of:

1. Why is this organisation going to adopt agile?
2. What is the transformation hypothesis?
3. The transformation strategy
4. Management of the change
5. Anticipated Results

The business case is possibly the first opportunity for the transformation team to start to create a "brand". The purpose of the brand is to articulate a single desirable future for the organisation and to create a flag or banner around people may gather and focus efforts on achieving the goals.

All too often, the leaders of a transformation use dry, technocratic language to explain the change and its rationale. However, in many successful endeavours, the leadership sets a challenging tone by translating the new strategic objectives into vivid, everyday language – so that everyone can see how their jobs contribute, and why each part of the change matters. It is this striking, often pictorial expression of intent which becomes the transformational brand. A brand which must be replayed as often as possible and used as a benchmark measure of progress and attainment.

A challenge for the Enterprise Agile Coach is that the business case will require numbers! Cost and benefit numbers.

The costs will primarily be driven by the strategy planned for the transformation, the number of teams and the geographic spread. These costs combined with the support plan drive the budget. Establishing who is going to train and support the teams will allow the Enterprise Agile Coach to prepare a budget. Will this support be provided by internal or external resources? How long will this support be needed? How will support be transitioned into business as usual and so on?

In establishing the benefit numbers, the Enterprise Agile Coach will need to forecast savings. For many, this may be uncomfortable. Yet sources of data are available.

As I outlined, one of the uses of the teams which have experimented with agile is to provide some benchmark data. If these teams saw a productivity gain or an improvement in time to market, then this data can be used and reflected in the business case. As a last resort, external benchmark data can be used as long as the coach puts a plan in place to replace the external data with internally generated results as soon as possible.

The essence of agile is clarity over the value generated. In my view, this principle should be as applicable to the agile transformation itself as it is to the agile initiatives.

Step 2 – The Transformation Sundial Recipe

Many leaders, and indeed experienced Agile Coaches, will have heard words like "we don't need a plan – we are agile" or "we can't give you a delivery date – we are agile". All coaches will understand the level of agile immaturity expressed in these purist statements! The transformation sundial is precisely that – it calibrates the transformation and tells you where you are against that calibration.

I prefer to use outcomes to calibrate the sundial with interim goals defined in the same way as a scrum team sets sprint goals. There is a temptation to plan in a highly agile way, with very little detail towards the later stages. I have found that stakeholders prefer headlines, as it gives them the comfort of a road map even if they recognise that this will change due to challenges, delays or unforeseen future circumstances.

For many reasons, operational, fiscal and human resource management, there are organisational requirements for budgets and expected timelines. It is therefore also essential that senior leadership understand the investment required and status of their transition, so they may understand the implications of the progress of the change on their strategic goals.

The strategy may also be to alter the organisation in increments and employ a gradual agile adoption. Whatever is decided, the outcome-based plan will consider the organisation's risk appetite combined with operational considerations when it comes to making the transition.

The Transformation Sundial Ingredients

The essence of the Formalisation stage is, therefore, to create a plan, a sundial, to develop the new organisation and ecosystem for the agile teams, indicating the path to transition to the new ways of working. It is critical that the transformational plan is outcome-based to maintain focus on these transitional goals and the building of capabilities.

The transformation sundial must be grounded in the fact that the organisation still must deliver services or products to its clients while this transition is happening. Risk management and cultural change are at the centre of this plan. The result is a unique plan for each organisation. Any evidence of wholesale "cookie cutting" should give executives cause for concern and should, therefore, be avoided by the Enterprise Agile Coach if possible.

Instead of being date focussed, this plan uses outcomes, objectives, or horizon goals to define the step changes in organisational. The concept is similar to the setting sprint goals in Scrum. The horizon goal may be linked to date but is also a statement of measurable capability. So, for example: "by March we (our organisation) will be able to deliver solutions using agile in France", or "by March we will be able to deliver all XYZ solutions using Agile". The horizon goal may have some scope limitations or guardrails such as: "without additional hiring" or "without automated testing". In addition, the outcome is supported by a success statement "we shall know we have succeeded by..." These success statements serve to illustrate progress or the status of the change initiative.

Like a sundial breaks hours into minutes, the horizon goal comprises several high-level activities; each of these activities listed as the transformation backlog. However, as people are unpredictable corrective or unexpected further actions may be necessary to reach the goal, and in this sense, the plan is adaptive.

So, the transformation sundial may be controlled in the same way as a sprint by prioritising the work items on a backlog and completing the critical, high-value or high-risk items as early as possible. Then adapting the activities until reaching the horizon goal.

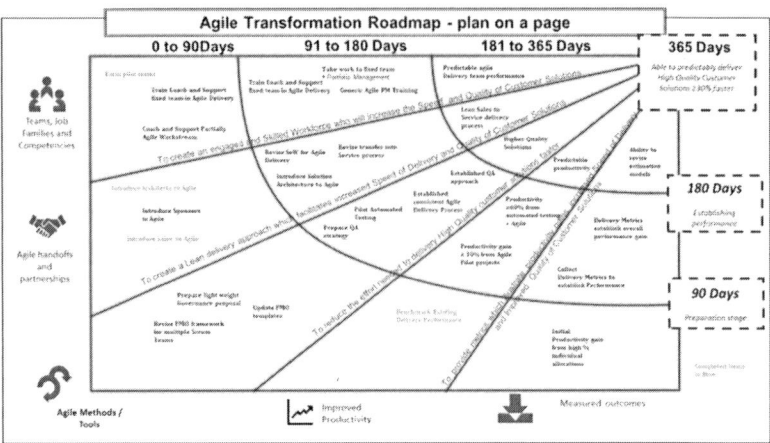

A transformation sundial with horizons

In the above example, 90-day boundaries are created for the immediate future with a single 180-day segment after that. Each zone represents a potential transformational work stream which has a conditional or outcome statement against which progress is measured. Behind this plan on a page will be a detailed outline for each zone headlining the principal elements of the new capability creation. Ideally, to manage status evaluations, these capabilities should be able to be evaluated using a binary condition; either it's done, or it's not.

The plan created needs to assess the ability of the organisation to absorb all of the changes. Too much and change fatigue may be encountered. Too little and executives may get frustrated by the pace of the transition.

The planning also needs to think through how the outcomes are to be monitored and measured. Without this vital aspect, senior executives are unable to establish if the risk to their organisation and customers is too significant or if their organisation is fit for purpose regarding the attainment of their strategic objectives.

If several teams, business functions or multiple organisational units are involved, big-room planning techniques may be employed to create the plan. In all cases, the Enterprise Agile Coach must resist the temptation to complete the plan themselves. Instead, inputs from stakeholders and champions during the planning session are used to create the roadmap or headline plan, even if the coach then fleshes out some of the details independently at a later point.

Once the organisation has a plan, the next question is likely to be who is going to do the work? In this regard, the Enterprise Agile Coach needs to act as a catalyst ensuring that the organisation retains ownership of its transformation and desired outcomes.

Ownership of the Plan Ingredients

The Enterprise Agile Coach needs to be extremely careful regarding the ownership of the transformation.

Many senior executives, when faced with a significant business problem, traditionally reach out for a branded consultancy and their challenge or situation is effectively resolved through the payment of consulting fees. In taking this action, the top executive has effectively passed the ownership from themselves to the consultancy. Yet, because agile is first and foremost about people, their organisation's DNA, a successful agile transformation cannot be dealt with hands-off in the same way.

The traditional consulting model of a senior consultancy leader accompanied by more junior consulting personnel typically excludes staff from the employing organisation from the detailed mechanics of the engagement. The consultancy operating model is generally based on the premise that transformation is done to the organisation by the consulting firm. Experience shows that if an agile transformation is conducted in this way, it will not stick and business agility if created, will erode quickly over time.

The behavioural change associated with agile adoption is significant, for senior executives, it invites inclusion and participation unseen by many since the earlier stages of their careers. For the junior population, it involves accepting levels of organisational authority. The executives must decide how much autonomy they wish to delegate or grant to their agile teams. At the team level, people must adapt to the new ways of working and understand the new responsibilities which they now share.

What is required, therefore, is the building of an agile capability which encourages, agile behaviour, organisational learning and evolution from within to create a long-lasting living outcome. The ownership, therefore, needs to be retained by the organisation as the derived agility is planned to last well beyond the activities of transformation.

The Plan – the Coaching Ingredients

An Enterprise Agile Coach needs to be constantly aware of the mindset of doing agile to an organisation; too much directional leadership and the coach will start to replicate the branded consultancy approach. Too little guidance and your stakeholders may feel that they are not getting what they need. Too much and you fall into the trap. This question of balance should be indirectly addressed with the stakeholders, probably while you involve them with the creation of the transformation plan. It could be phrased to answer a "what do you expect from me", the coaching contracting question when discussing roles and responsibilities during planning or earlier.

Due to the wide-ranging impact of an agile transformation, the plan must be clear. It must give a clear picture of the objectives, and it needs to be capable of illustrating progress towards the desired capabilities. As we have linked the agile introduction to strategic imperatives, it is crucial that senior executives understand the activity progress so that they can make strategic decisions based upon the capability developed and assess if they are yet able to deliver their strategic goals.

Broad and Shallow or Narrow and Deep Strategies

There are broadly two strategies to consider in creating the plan. I shall call them Broad and Shallow and Narrow and Deep.

In a typical large development organisation, maybe in a bank or telecoms provider. Senior management layer at the top of the organisation is in contact with the very senior management or the owners. They are in daily touch with the business and the market realities. They identify the strategy and will have probably generated or at least approved the rationale for changing to agile ways of working.

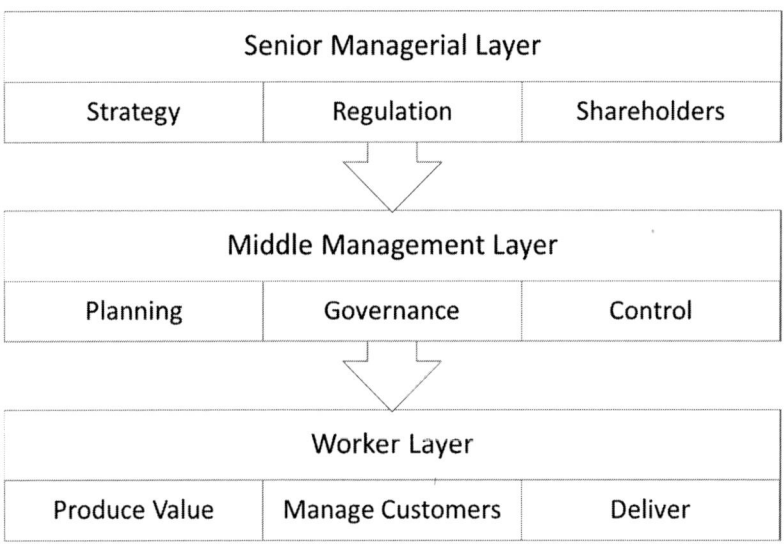

Layers of organisation with associated responsibilities

At the bottom layer, there are the worker bees; they produce the work and create most of the business value. These people are in tune with the technical realities of the organisation as they encounter the organisational issues on an almost daily basis.

The middle organisational layer from an agile coaching perspective is the most challenging. These individuals are dealing mostly with internal questions of control, coordination, intermediation, analysis and execution. It is this middle layer, the jam in the sandwich, which is often the most resistant to change.

The middle layer is always the layer most threatened by the adoption of agile. The source of middle-management power is often detailed knowledge of processes or some other specialist knowledge. This level of influence is usually removed, or significantly modified by agile adoption. Hence the need for the middle management layer to be convinced of the benefits of agile.

Middle management often needs as much of the attention of the Enterprise Agile Coach and the teams during a transformation. Strategies are, therefore required to encourage acceptance and adoption by the middle layer. I have used piloting with PDCA cycles to involve middle management. I have included this group in the problem-solving Executive Action Teams, in the process redesign and organisational realignment. Eventually, however, the question always becomes does this middle manager wish to learn or experiment with new ways of working or not?

In planning a transformation, there are two very different strategies; a horizontal, broad and shallow approach, or a vertical, deep and narrow approach. Both involve working with the middle layer but in different ways.

A horizontal, broad and shallow approach involves mass training efforts and collective adoption across many products or development teams. It means making a large-scale change to the processes and controls used by middle management. It suffers from needing to convince a potentially large number of people, and consequently, their working practices. New methods must, therefore, be well defined before implementing widespread change.

Broad and shallow	Narrow and deep
• Transitions a lot of people at one time	• Transitions individual teams at one time
• Less control	• High degree of control
• Bigger change management implications	• Change managed by PDCA and piloting
• Result less fundamental change to the organisation	• Results in a growing adoption of fundamental change

With a broad and shallow transformation approach, working with the middle-management layer is more complicated. Broad and shallow requires a lot of process redesign and implementation, resulting in the Enterprise Agile Coach managing multiple workstreams simultaneously.

Broad and Shallow Ingredients

The broad and shallow approach is intended to bring about agility for the masses without necessarily changing from a functional organisation to a cross-functional, multi-disciplined teams organisational structure. Broad and shallow is useful when there is a significant appetite for change but insufficient senior managerial demand for improving the entire organisation. Typically, a broad and shallow strategy would involve "sheep dipping" large numbers of people in agile training and expecting them to be able to use this training when they start an agile activity. Yet based upon experience, it also means dealing with resistance from the middle management layer on a significant scale.

Broad and shallow approaches create energy from people who want to do the right thing. From a coaching perspective, it generates a significant workload. The coaching activities lead to opening many minds across an organisation, accelerated learning and deeper collective understanding. In the plan, schemes need to be developed harness and engage these minds so that the productively move the transformation.

In a broad and shallow approach, wholesale changes to the organisational processes and structures are required. Failure to do these level of change exposes a risk that all these newly energised people hit the anti-agile patterns embedded in the organisation resulting in a loss of the freshly generated inertia. Without significant top-level support, broad and shallow strategies tend to be less successful, people quickly lose energy and people get frustrated by operational obstacles and rigidity.

Narrow and Deep Ingredients

With a vertical strategy, a narrow and deep focus, you may take one product at a time, or team first achieve success and then move on. The number of teams or activities transitioning at one time is limited, gradually proving the success and minimising organisational disruption. From a coaching perspective, this is a far more straightforward approach to dealing with middle management resistance as the initial transition has limited scope.

A narrow and deep strategy allows the coach; to focus on a small number of teams. To identify and resolve systemic or organisational challenges as they go. It will enable controlled adoption of new tooling or the technology often required when changing to agile ways of working.

Working with the middle management layer is easier because widespread change can be proceeded by the piloting of process changes using PDCA cycles. Middle management can be involved in revisions. A narrow and deep is often needed to prove then embed the new ways of working, resulting in less chance of regressing to previous practices.

Identifying the Anti-Agile Patterns

When creating a plan, the Enterprise Agile Coach must consider aspects of the organisations which may limit success or delay the transformation. During the situational analysis, the agile coach needs to consider the working practices, managerial behaviour and culture, which will prevent agile ways of working. I will call these the anti-agile patterns.

By anti-agile patterns, I refer to practices such as the annual budgeting process, the project or investment approval process, change governance and status reporting. Typically, these processes impose rules and necessitate behaviours based on a waterfall or traditional solution delivery approaches. Historically, many of these mechanisms were introduced based on the belief that managing process increased the probability of success. These practices, therefore, represent the perceived understanding and the knowledge of what was needed to deliver solutions in the organisation. The Enterprise Agile Coach needs to plan to identify and nullify these patterns, or the resultant agile ways of working will either be blocked or be sub-optimal.

Another focus area is management behaviour; agile steps away from the command-and-control culture and the scientific management approaches on which many organisations rely. Agile introduces a self-managed, continuously improving organisation shown in the mid-to-late twentieth century by both academia and business practice to increase the productivity and the efficiency of teams. However, if the command-and-control patterns are allowed to persist, then the results from the investment in agile will be sub-optimal.

When creating the plan, the coach needs to allow time and mechanisms to identify and nullify each of the anti-agile patterns, which may frustrate the transformation.

Following the Finances Recipe

One good source of establishing the anti-agile patterns I have found is to map out how initiatives get funded, resourced and started. This chain of events is different in every organisation, but it is here where some of the agile blockers exist. For example, in one client, the Finance function would only release funding for an activity once a detailed project initiation document and comprehensive project Gantt Chart was prepared. As a coach, I had to counter this insistence before I could lead the team into Agile Requirements Management and Release Planning.

Conversely, when looking at ways of enabling agile, then the funding and activity mobilising sequence is often an excellent place to make changes to enforce the agile behaviours. Most Sponsors and teams will adopt new ways of working if it means their pet initiative will get the necessary funding!

Systemic Challenges Recipe

Another area to consider when creating the plan are systemic challenges. These could include an inappropriate toolset or a lack of test environments to allow teams to adopt continuous delivery or automated testing techniques.

Systemic challenges could be operational, organisational or managerial. For example, if testing environments were limited or shared for waterfall solution delivery, then capacity may not exist to allow teams to test throughout the delivery lifecycle using agile.

Or if, senior or mid-level managers were appointed as technical leaders due to the many years' service or based upon their acquaintance with the traditional working practices. These individuals, suddenly encountering: the immediacy of decision making required by a Scrum, the pressure of dealing with the delivery teams on almost a daily basis, or dramatic changes to the technology and process landscape, could feel immensely threatened and concerned about their future.

It is the Enterprise Agile Coach's role to support the process changes and coach all of the individuals impacted. Some people will, of course, adapt. Nevertheless, to be brutally honest, others will not be able to cope and will need a change in their responsibilities.

Systemic Challenges Ingredients

As the agile approaches mature, the type of the systemic challenges faced by the teams and the coaches will change. The systemic problems are where the adaptive nature of the agile transformation plan comes into play.

If one role of the Enterprise Agile Coach is to remain relevant to the teams they support, then they will need to keep abreast of the current challenges faced by the teams. The retrospective is one source of information which when taken across several teams will allow the coach to identify systemic issues. Of course, some of the challenges outlined in the retrospective will be specific team orientated. However, some will be systemic in nature and require influence outside of the team for resolution. It is these challenges which need the attention of the Enterprise Agile Coach until they are resolved.

As such it is a role of the agile coach to be an individual where Scrum Masters can feel safe in identifying external challenges, with the knowledge that the concerns of the team will be progressed, identified if not resolved. If there are deep-rooted problems in the organisation which cannot be helped by agile, then the coach needs to call these out as implementing agile might lead to more frustration rather than resolving the challenges. (See the section on Executive Action Teams for more details.)

Planning the Communications Recipe

The key tool used by the Enterprise Agile Coach to help the organisation navigate transformational change is communications. The stakeholder analysis and communications planning seem to be an area where most agile coaches make improvements. So, I have added a little more detail to the section. For the preparation of communications or transformational interactions, I use a four-stage model:

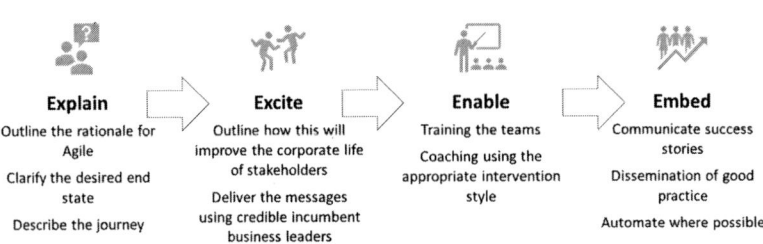

Explain	Excite	Enable	Embed
Outline the rationale for Agile	Outline how this will improve the corporate life of stakeholders	Training the teams	Communicate success stories
Clarify the desired end state	Deliver the messages using credible incumbent business leaders	Coaching using the appropriate intervention style	Dissemination of good practice
Describe the journey			Automate where possible

The Communications Plan

Explain – as an Enterprise Agile Coach, you may be aware of the need for the change and how it benefits the organisation. So may your transformation team and those directly involved. However, all the stakeholders and the teams impacted may not be aware of the rationale for this information. The activities in this first part of the communication plan enable each person affected to understand what's coming and how it impacts them.

Excite – Clarify individual and collective benefits for all stakeholders and stakeholder groups. What's in it for them is a critical element of the excite part of the communication. How will this transformation make their corporate life better? It is a question all stakeholders will be asking themselves. How is this different from what has gone before? It is good to think the communications through from the benefit to the individual perspective and ensure that this part of the message is clearly stated from the outset.

Tempting although it is, these messages need to come from incumbent senior leaders in the organisation and not from the coach or the transformation team. It is part of the organisation owning the transformation. It is also essential that credible senior executives deliver these messages. The senior leader should be someone who has rapport and credibility with those targeted to receive the information. It is equally vital that these senior leaders are well briefed and prepared. A coach cannot expect senior executives to talk about the change unless they are fully informed, understand the strategic imperatives and are committed to the change journey.

Enable – Activities included in this area of the communications plan include the training and the opportunities for feedback from the teams and stakeholders. The Enterprise Agile Coach must remember that communication is a two-way process. Throughout the communications plan, opportunities for input from those impacted need to be included in addition to activities relating to the dissemination of information. Listening opportunities can be created through communities of practice, through lunch and learn sessions, walk-in clinics and through chat rooms using collaboration tools such as Slack.

Embed – These are the communications designed to help the new ways of working "stick" so new ways of working become second nature and the regular practice for business as usual. Types of communication valued by teams are success stories, good practices and examples of how the new ways of working have helped the business move towards the achievement of its strategic goals.

These communications should have elements which point to the progress towards the targeted metrics or business baselines. Again, the credibility of the individual presenting the information is critical. These embed messages have the most significant impact if they are performed by those who had the experiences first-hand rather than those not directly involved relaying stories.

Communications Ingredients

It is essential to make as much of the communication face to face as possible. Communicating in person may not be as efficient as email or broadcast announcements or twitter, but the human side of the exchange is so powerful. Body language, voice inflexions and facial expressions matter in getting the whole message across to the recipients. Telling "war stories" responding to questions, even engaging in emotional debates, can help clear the air and keep the rumour mill in check.

Make sure that those delivering the communications are well prepared and have prepared ways of helping those delivering the messages should they receive unforeseen inputs or questions.

Create a cascade-down feedback-up, loop possibly using the planned communications to cascade with the agile champions or ambassadors feeding back.

Make sure all the messages are aligned, have a purpose and are consistent. So, for example, that the initial communication perhaps a town hall meeting, is reinforced and expanded by subsequent department meetings. These same communications are then reinforced through the activities with the champions and communities of practice into individual team meetings.

The messages should get more specific as you get into the team level, but they need to remain consistent from the top all the way to the team level. As issues, questions and details resolved during the implementation, feedback loops should communicate back to the transformation team about what is working and what still needs to be adjusted.

It may seem pointless to say it but keep communicating. Transformational communications over time will become part of the business-as-usual communication patterns. Communicating just once doesn't work! Repetition and reinforcement of messaging are all critical. Think of how often the same advertisement is broadcast on TV on the same evening and you will start to see how much effort you need to devote to the communications plan. Constant communication helps sustain and coordinate the transformational effort. People need to know that the new ways of working are still important and that they should continue their efforts on the change.

Lastly, as when coaching a team, the Enterprise Agile Coach should – listen, listen, listen!

All of these communications strategies are based upon a thorough and careful stakeholder analysis which is undertaken during the situational analysis activity and has ongoing revision.

Managing Stakeholder Recipe

Stakeholder analysis is a technique often misused by many. I have seen instances where a stakeholder analysis is performed only to be placed on a shelf and never referred to again! A stakeholder analysis is a fundamental tool used by the Enterprise Agile Coach to plan and define which people need communications, intervention and to adopt change.

In this context, stakeholders are all of those who need to be considered in achieving the agile transformation goals. It will include; groups of people in locations who will be converting to agile ways of working, individuals, functions or departments within the organisation who support or administer those groups of people, external individuals, roles or departments who have influence over the individuals or teams delivering using agile.

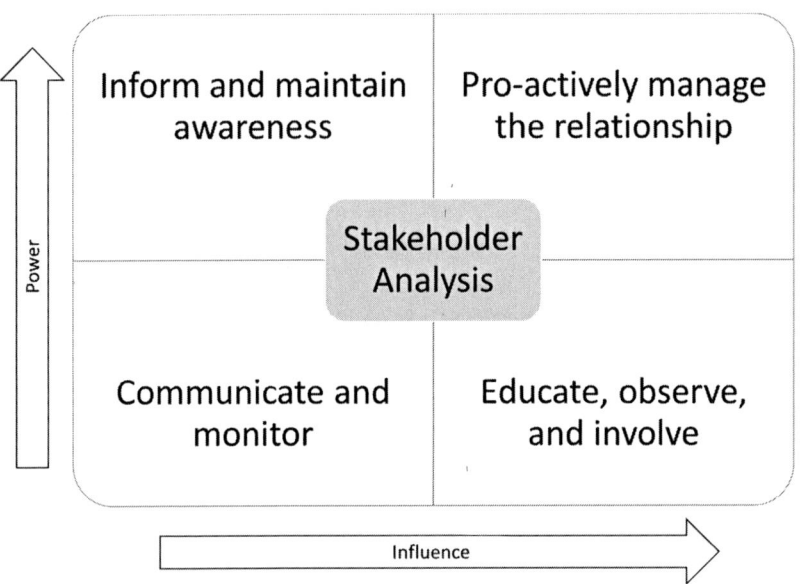

The starting point is to undertake a stakeholder analysis.

Stakeholders with high power and high interest are significant stakeholders who are deeply involved in the initiative. These primary stakeholders will typically share in the results of the transformation. Many indeed may also have an active part to play in the organisational, process and technical changes required. The Enterprise Agile Coach will be concerned to be actively communicating and ensuring this group's expectations are well-managed.

Stakeholders with high-power but low-influence must also be kept satisfied. They often can derail or block the change initiative over seemingly minor issues. This group needs to be educated on the stages and progression of the transformation. The Enterprise Agile Coach should observe and involve this group as often as possible.

Stakeholders with low-power but high-influence must be kept informed. As they can have a significant impact, it is essential to keep them informed and aligned with the transformational goals.

It is often forgotten, but the views and concerns of Stakeholders with low-power and low-influence should not be overlooked. Perhaps without the same verve as the other groups, they should still be engaged and provided with communication so that their opinions can be monitored. This investment is just in case they have genuine concerns which should be addressed but also because as the transformation evolves some of this group could become more directly involved and could, therefore, amplify their concerns in the future.

Informing, influencing and seeking feedback are essential elements with all groups. It is the degrees of each of these activities which varies between groups. The workload this represents should not be underestimated, and it is here where the role of an agile champion can come into play.

Communications Plan Template

The communication plan outlines the activity, the objective of the communication and the timing of the intervention. See example below:

Activity	Objectives	Audience	When
Senior Executives Briefing	A short workshop targeted at giving a broad introduction to agile and why this transformation is taking place. Suggested agenda: 1. How agile enables the organisational strategy 2. A general overview of agility (to include a glossary of agile terms) 3. The anticipated benefits 4. The impacts in summary on, Operations, Marketing, Sales and Finance 5. An overview of the transformational roadmap and expected financial results or business case	C-suite plus one level	Month two

Cross Organisation Communications	A communication to as many made by middle and senior management regarding the rationale and potential impact of adopting agile. in addition to outlining the goals and context for the transformation, you should also include key planning details such as: • The overall timeline. • The learning goals and key messages. • The stakeholders, who and how to involve (for example, in this communication, you can outline any initial milestones, such as implementation dates or agile piloting activities or trails of new tooling. Suggestions: This communication will probably be in the form of a meeting or a written guide from the Agile change leaders (you) to managers and team leaders (recipients). If you decide to have middle managers conduct some of the session, you need to provide them with appropriate worksheets and instructions how to participate and share the results from their conversations, or they will not become part of the transformation team. The following is a summary	All those impacted or affected	

	of the potential resources they will need. 1. Provide background advice and information which the briefing managers can use to inform employees regarding agile. Reiterate key messages, evidence, business rationale and other essential components. 2. Provide managers with suggestions and ideas for how coaching and support will be provided to teams. These can include: a. The coaching activities (workshops, exercises, training). b. The use of agile champions. c. Questions and Answers (prepare your team to answer questions raised by staff). 3. An outline of the opportunities for personal growth allowing managers to respond with career suggestions and opportunities for individuals. 4. Provide measurement or goal suggestions for later discussions.		

	a. a worksheet detailing key measures at various implementation times)		
Training plan announcement	Call to action outlining the dates for formal training courses	All those impacted or affected	Month three

Step 3 – Support Model Recipe

The third step is to define in detail the support provision for transitioning teams. As the new ways of working are adopted, the teams will require training and coaching support. Support is labour intensive, and in most circumstances, it is impractical or a high-risk strategy to change the whole organisation at once. The support plan typically involves; trainers, coaches, champions and the PMO.

Having attended the training, most teams initially struggle with the practical application of their newly learned skills on an initiative for the first time. They, therefore, need someone, a coach or a champion, someone external to the team on who they can rely for practical advice.

The coach is an experienced agilist who has the skill to share their expertise with an agile team. The agile coach is also responsible for providing feedback and advice to the new agile teams and assists teams who want to reach and perform their work at a higher level of productivity. An alternative is an Agile Champion.

A champion differs from a coach in terms of depth of practical agile expertise. A champion brings specialist knowledge of how agile culture or practices impact a particular business area. So, for example, there could be an agile champion in sales dealing with writing proposals or negotiating contracts.

The agile champion or ambassador is someone who can have detailed oversight of the agile processes and how the new ways of working are impacting their area of expertise or sphere. The purists may argue that everything is down to the team, and I agree with this assertion. However, when it comes to the redefinition of processes outside of the team, and this is central in an agile transformation, then I have learned those subject matter experts, champions in a particular business area or process owners provide essential input to a team.

Agile Champion Recipe

How can a coach identify or grow agile champions or ambassadors? I use a four-step approach:

1. An initial communication or workshop for people throughout the organisation where people learn about what it means to be agile. The agile team, general principles, the scrum process and value. This communication also explores the role of the Agile Champion and how they may be called upon to provide specialist knowledge to teams in transition.
2. Identification and selection. The champions need to be someone particularly interested in agile, but also have credibility within their specialist sphere. Often the coach needs to overcome fear or trepidation of the champion with stepping into the unknown. Sometimes a detailed conversation is required to help the potential champion explore how they think agile may impact or alter their sphere.
3. The provision of generic agile training for each of the Champions; this is most likely a formal class, but Champions don't need to have agile certification unless they want it! Training is followed by the exploration of how agile will impact a business area or process for the champion's area building their expertise.
4. Lastly, the coach needs to cultivate the champion helping them with areas of understanding

Step 4 – Creating the new WOW – the framework fixation

In this step, the Enterprise Agile Coach acts mainly as an agile consultant, the PMO and champions assisted by coach creates a definition of the new ways of working (the new WOW!). In many instances, there is a temptation to say oh we are going to do Scrum, or we will adopt DSDM or let's go SAFe, but the organisation will need ways of working which allows it to achieve its strategic goals. This relevance rarely comes from a framework straight out-of-the-box.

People want to know how to do agile and think that a framework will provide this. So, the pervading idea at the beginning of a transformation is often that the teams must adopt a particular framework, and their agility is guaranteed. Sometimes this view is encouraged by a PMO. Precisely, the reason why it is essential that the Enterprise Agile Coach aligns the PMO and treats them as an ally in the transformation.

This fixation of frameworks has two adverse side-effects which could cause much of the poor or fake agile we see out there. The first is that there will rarely be a framework which fits the organisational needs perfectly. Secondly is that in unthinkingly adopting a specific framework, the organisation is subtly teaching people to be followers taking away the empowerment element which agile emphasises.

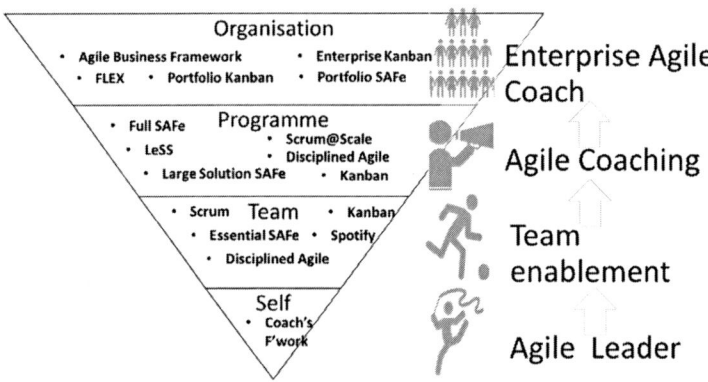

Aligning frameworks to operational layers

Many scaling agile frameworks look to solve the problems associated with larger teams. Quite often organisations get unduly focused on the question of how the frameworks differ or perhaps choosing which one will work best for them.

There are, of course, excellent parts within all these frameworks (and perhaps others not mentioned here). Yet, implementing the XYZ framework should not be the goal; because every organisation is different, and there isn't a "one size fits all" agile approach. Furthermore, there is not likely to be one ever! Instead, the Enterprise Agile Coach should treat each framework as a set of resources from which to create a specific model, a particular methodology which fits the context of the organisation. Approximately, one in five organisations follow their own tailored methods rather than those commercially available.

Tailoring of the Framework Recipe

As there is no one single best approach to scaling agile delivery which suits all organisations, we probably should look at how we can make use of the frameworks.

Each agile framework has prescribed solutions at each layer of the operational model, as shown in the diagram. Each framework "out-of-the-box" has gaps, processes, procedures, roles which need definition before agile becomes a workable enterprise solution.

While piloting these gaps typically are not significant; it is when industrialising the agile practices, they will require to be changed. The long-term success of the tailored organisational approach to agile will depend mainly upon its fitness for purpose alignment with culture and its ability to adapt to changing operational circumstances.

So, the Enterprise Agile Coach must assist the organisation in tailoring a framework into an agile methodology which they can make their own. It may be that it is necessary to take components or approaches from more than one framework and adapt them for organisational use.

Role Mapping Recipe

Unless you are dealing with a brand-new organisation, people in your target agile community already have job descriptions and critical measures possibly attached to bonus schemes which need to be countered or adapted. As part of the transformation, a new definition of roles and responsibilities will need to be defined. This definition needs to map the new agile roles on to the existing job descriptions. This mapping should consider that the Product Owner and Scrum Master are potentially hats rather than job titles. It also needs to cover areas like governance, stakeholder management and the broader organisational requirements.

Building the Agile Ecosystem

As organisations become more agile and customer-focused, they are shifting from traditional, functional structures to interconnected, flexible teams. A new organisational model is on the rise: a "network or team of teams" in which companies build and empower their teams to work on specific business initiatives or challenges. These networks of teams are aligned and coordinated with operations and information centres. However, to be effective, they often need a new ecosystem of training, tools, procedures and working practices.

It is unlikely that the new ecosystem will be designed and implemented as a single event. That would not be very agile! Instead, the Enterprise Agile Coach should expect to enable a team to set an overall direction of travel with a series of delivery increments just like the preparation of an agile release plan used by a Scrum team.

While agile working practices are essential to the transformation, some require tooling to be fully effective. The Enterprise Agile Coach should be aware of these constraints and make them explicit in the agile transformation plan.

Quality Assurance Recipe

One such area where tooling is almost certain to be required is quality assurance and testing. Agile practices provide teams and individuals with responsibility and ownership for the quality of the solutions they develop. Enabling teams to manage solution quality while iterating, churning code and deciphering customer requirements. In this way, with collaboration and flexibility, teams can deliver innovative applications. Yet, this innovation often depends upon having the relevant tooling to increase efficiency.

Agile QA helps to proactively address issues and potential bugs within a solution during the development cycles. It can also help address functionality, performance or security issues. Agile QA will not only ensure the stability of the application but also bring down the testing efforts once a solution lands in the hands of customers. In this way, developers can move ahead without dealing relentlessly with pending issues or rework.

With shorter goals, development goals and with smaller targets. Agile QA needs to align and become much faster and more dynamic in nature. A result-oriented Agile QA approach can make all the possible difference for teams driving quickly towards the end objective. Testers and developers do work together, but delivering specific results makes them work more cohesively.

Step 5 – Train the Team Members

An organisation adopting agile is often attempting to deliver solutions more quickly, or make more efficient use of scarce resources, or make improvements in the quality of the outputs delivered. Sometimes, the goal of the agile transformation is to make improvements in all three dimensions!

The starting point is often a training needs analysis. A training needs analysis allows you to decide what type of internal or external training you require. It can be a challenge to make sure you are picking the correct instruction for each stakeholder, ensuring that they each get the most benefit from the training selected. There are broadly three steps in the process:

1. Decide on the skill sets which will be required. This analysis means looking at every job role separately and considering things like the different departments or levels of seniority.

2. Evaluate current capabilities. This step involves a systematic, albeit lightweight, evaluation concerning the skills identified in the first stage of this process and the existing capabilities of the people transitioning to agile.

3. Highlight the gap in skills needed. With the difference in skills established and quantified, then training be can be procured or develop targeted at closing the gap and equipping teams and stakeholders with the skills they require.

Coach and Support Teams' Recipes

It is common to find that off-the-shelf externally provided training will not cover all the required elements that you need. For example, it is highly likely that training the new internal processes will be necessary. This internal necessity will not be available in commercially delivered generic training. On the other hand, some generic training may give an overview of the new roles and the agile principles and serve as an introduction. Scrum Master training could be an example of this. Online training is available from most of the agile framework sources, and this resource agile coach should explore these and make appropriate recommendations. Most framework providers emphasis certification which may be relevant. However, certification may be deemed as an unnecessary expense in some organisations with a limited training budget. Certification or not the training delivered needs to cover the training needs and raise the levels of competency so that people can succeed.

Most likely is that you will use a blended training approach with some computer-based training, some face-to-face classroom sessions supported by individual coaching sessions provided by the agile coaches and others.

Training needs do not just stop with the teams. Other stakeholders such as the PMO and initiative sponsors should be included in the training needs analysis.

Coaching and Supporting the Sponsor's Recipe

Adopting an agile ethos involves a significant cultural change for the organisation, and none is more impacted than the senior managers who sponsor initiatives. In making the agile transition, as a coach, you need to take the time to establish executive trust in the new practices. Senior executives are used to using specific tools and seeing reports which allow them to interpret the health of the activity for which they are responsible. With agile, these tools and reports will change in content and format. These senior executives often require training and mentoring from the Enterprise Agile Coach in the same way as the development team.

The focus of agile on the value produced is of great benefit to a sponsor who typically has responsibility for the delivery of the benefits identified in the business case for an initiative. I have found a benefit to amplify the value focus for senior leaders. However, an Enterprise Agile Coach needs to be aware of the downside for sponsors. If the development team concentrates on the creation of value and delivers; then, equally, sponsors are required to realise any benefits identified in the business case. Sometimes this exposes any fantasy benefits a consequence which may cause a sponsor to resist transitioning to agile!

I have observed that a combination of agile delivery with benefits tracking has encouraged organisations to improve the quality of business cases and to increase the value realised from their investments in change.

Coaching Sponsor's Ingredients

The move away from a command-and-control culture to a self-managed team has several impacts. Including:

- A self-managed team will seek clarity regarding scope and requirements. Overcoming the challenge of fuzzy requirements experienced in many waterfall projects. Sometimes the team requesting clarification is seen in a negative light by sponsors.
- That the sponsor must adapt his or her traditional management style to allow for the agile self-managed ethos, bluntly, self-management means delegating approval responsibility one or two levels down the management hierarchy. Sometimes, sponsors find releasing their authority difficult, and they attempt to retain the final say.

- Agile delivery employs businesspeople and solution developers working in collaboration throughout the activity. Collaboration challenges organisational silos and "them and us" behaviours which may be cultural behaviour of the past. Sometimes, sponsors have encouraged silo working for political reasons. Breaking down organisational silos can be uncomfortable for some sponsors.

As can be seen, these impacts frequently present personal challenges to Sponsors which an Enterprise Agile Coach needs to address similar to the issues faced by a development team.

Sponsors also need to be aware and comfortable with the new ways of working. Some sponsors struggle with the agile emphasis on "just enough" documentation rather than fully defined requirements before solution delivery starts. Some sponsors may feel relieved that they no longer need to study a tome and give it their approval. Other may feel nervous that they cannot see what is to be delivered and this begs the question, what is "just enough"?

Agile release planning also causes sponsors concern. If they previously sought comfort with a detailed project plan giving them a line of sight from start to completion, then they need reassurance regarding agile planning and estimation.

Agile uses frequent sprint reviews or show and tell sessions as a means of illustrating progress. In coaching sponsors, it is often necessary to lead them through the Scrum ceremonies so that they appreciate the alternative, powerful means of control which are provided by agile.

It also said that agile teams also welcome changing requirements, even at late stages in the solution delivery. This statement often needs to be placed in context for a sponsor. Agile processes typically harness positive change for additional value created or the customer's competitive advantage. Some sponsors may find this encouraging. Yet, it is often necessary to explain in detail how scope control works in an agile activity and that budgets for agile activities are rarely completely elastic!

In all, senior leaders typically need as much support in transitioning to agile. They deserve a focus from an Enterprise Agile Coach who has the necessary credibility to work with C-suite individuals. In a recent assignment, in a highly hierarchical organisation, we had a coach aligned just with senior leaders. This coach did not initially work with development teams for political segregation reasons. When the top team became more comfortable with their agile culture, we widened the remit of our C-level coach to support the total span of the organisation.

Step 6 – Mobilise

The mobilisation step is where the application of the transformation strategy; narrow and deep or broad and shallow comes into reality. It is when the organisation starts to think about the impact of the agile ways of working on the portfolio of activities. There is a form of go, no-go decision then transition starts.

Mobilisation is a time to check the readiness of coaches, champions, trainers and assess that the PMO can move from training into support. Mobilisation is a critical part of the communications plan; the transformation team will wish to explain their roll-out strategy and should look for every opportunity to broadcast success stories. This delivery of this information is an essential part of the transformation, and with these communications, senior stakeholders start to see the results of their investment in transitioning to agile.

However, from a coaching perspective, these communications will also generate pressure from senior leadership to either go faster or to widen the approach; and is why the transition to agile needs careful consideration of the operational risk involved in the transition.

Step 7 – Transition of In-Flight activities

Unless an organisation is a start-up, then all will have in-flight activities in the portfolio. The portfolio management process usually provides enough data to allow decisions to be made regarding the roll-out of new ways of working.

Having the entire organisation begin to use a new delivery process, that is not mature, and in which the people are inexperienced, may confuse and ultimately may result in a spectacular failure. If the Enterprise Agile Coach starts to transition the organisation too early and makes a mistake resulting in one or more initiative failures, you will naturally increase the opportunity for change resistance. So it pays to be extremely careful regarding the transition of in-flight activities.

Taking the narrow and deep approach, the agile coach should select activities that are very early in the life cycle as a transition to agile candidate project.

Candidate Activities to Transition Ingredients

Unless an organisation is a start-up, then the transformation needs to cater for the transition of in-flight activities. Large organisations will have many different projects, initiatives, portfolios and programmes, on the go at any one time. All the initiatives will be at various lifecycle stages, including activities which are starting up and others concluding.

The question most Enterprise Agile Coach's face during transformation is which candidate activities to consider agile delivery from traditional means.

I have found some use agile scorecards; however, these date from about ten years ago, and I sense that they may have a "stay traditional" orientation. In a recent transformation, I found that if I considered the training and the willingness of stakeholders to adopt agile, then the result from the scorecard for every activity was "suitable for agile"!

I there created a process flow which balanced the desire of the stakeholders to change, with the risks of delivering crucial activities to customers using new ways of working.

In my customer, a regulated environment, a checkpoint process was required. The checkpoints were necessary so that executives could, if challenged by the regulator, prove the oversight and rigour embedded in the process.

We set four over-arching suitability criteria for an agile candidate activity:

1. We would consider for agile if the effort and time were spent on transitioning an in-flight project to agile, then we would be able to impact the activity and recover this effort and time delay – there had to be a payback.
2. We would consider agile if the relationship with the customer would allow changing the project approach
3. We would consider for agile of the waterfall project was in green status and not challenged.
4. We would consider for agile when we had sufficient training and coaching capacity to be able to support the transitioning team(s).

Selecting candidate activities to transition to agile was subject to several additional rules:

1. All unstarted activities, subject to the availability of coaches, would be considered for agile delivery.
2. Waterfall projects which had passed the detailed design stage would continue to be delivered by traditional methods.
3. In transitioning from waterfall to agile, we would not rework any existing documentation except where there were gaps. For example, the project charter had more information than the current Project Initiation Document (PID). We filled the differences by creating an agile addendum to the PID.

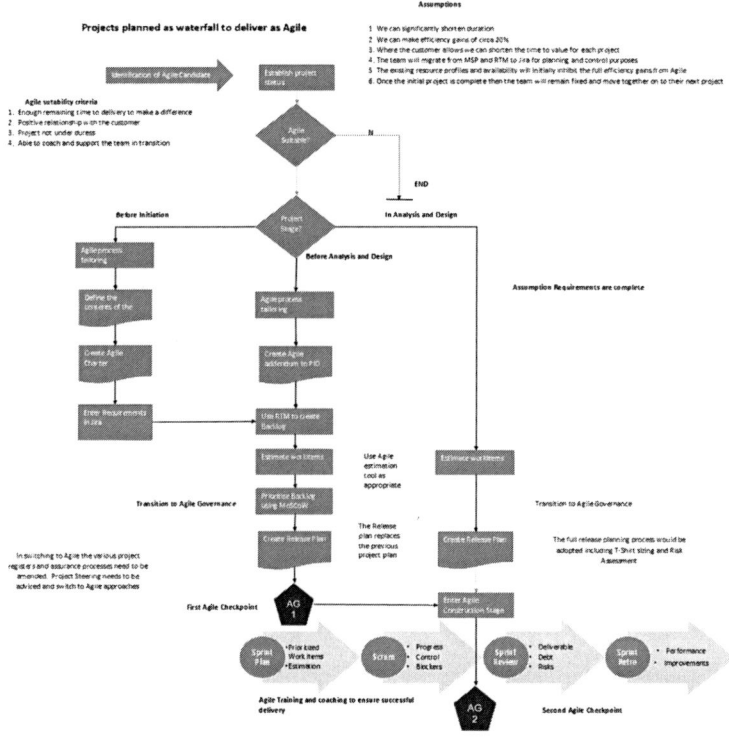

Transition to Agile decision Tree

4. Project in the waterfall Initiation stage after team training would move to an agile lifecycle joining at the point of agile process tailoring and continue through requirements elucidation.
5. Projects before analysis and design will have established the high-level scoping requirements but need the agile process tailoring step and require a project charter addendum before continuing into construction.

6. For waterfall projects in Analysis and Design and high-level scoping requirements have been completed, then these projects could be converted to agile activities and the point of splitting requirements into epics and stories. These activities would then create a backlog and start estimating and Sprint planning in their Sprint cycles.

Step 8 – Coach and Support

This step is where everything comes together, and the coaches can make use of recipes from all sections of this book!

Coaching and supporting the organisation can be a mammoth task. If the Enterprise Agile Coach has organised sufficient training sessions, identified and trained agile champions or ambassadors, and worked with the PMO to transition their processes from waterfall to agile, then the Enterprise Agile Coach is not the only source of training and support for the teams.

The goal of this step is to equip agile teams with the practical experience, the tools and on-going support so that they will be able to use their agile delivery process to its full potential. Using the coaching plan recipe and team health check recipe identified earlier in this book, the coach aims to increase maturity over time to the point of coaching redundancy.

Allocation of Coaches to Teams' Recipe

The assignment of agile coaches to teams is often a critical element and one which is essential when the transformation sundial. The crucial consideration is the agile maturity of the team, which dictates how many working hours the coach needs to support the team. Typically, a coach may help one team start-up at a time and once the team has moved onto the second or third iteration then the coaching workload usually significantly reduces as the need to observe the detail of the daily Scrum diminishes the coaching focus switches instead to planning and control and the use of metrics. In this way, an agile coach may support three or four teams if they are not all in start-up mode at the same time.

Allocating the right amount of time to coach the organisation and teams is critical. Over allocation of coaching may stunt the growth of agile capabilities as teams and individuals can defer or lean on the coach. Insufficient allocation of coaching time and the pace of the transition may suffer, the teams may struggle and be unable to deliver solutions predictably.

The allocation of coaches to teams relies upon three recipes from the Hors d'oeuve section of this book; the Coaching Contract recipe, the Team Health Check recipe and the Reflective Practice recipe. Using a combination of these techniques will allow a coach and team to decide how much coaching time they require and this can determine the allocations.

Communities of practice

Communities of practice (COP) are groups of individuals who engage in the process of collective learning and sharing of experiences. The COP is a useful construct for an Enterprise Agile Coach as they can feedback the effects of the transition to agile. They provide a means of listening to the broader community. The new roles, new practices, new tools all generate interest in the impacted community and creates a desire for learning. Communities of practice are, therefore, groups of people who form to share a concern or a passion for something they do and learn how to do it better as they interact.

Communities of practice don't just happen; they require planning, effort and support, from the Enterprise Agile Coach. However, the coach should adopt a stance which encourages the COP to be self-sufficient in the medium-term. The COP is a communications vehicle which is extensively used by the Enterprise Agile Coach to inform and to listen. Problems aired in the COP forum can be validated and acted upon as necessary. An Executive Action Team may be mobilised when systemic challenges are identified.

The PMO As a Catalyst

In a traditional waterfall organisation, the PMO sometimes acts as the process police, guarding against the business impact of risk. The PMO is typically a team of people who wish to see baseline plans, enforce quality gates, maintain raid logs and RAG statuses and create summary reporting packs for senior leadership. In transformation, these same people are a powerful resource which should be engaged. They have knowledge, contacts and an unrivalled organisational awareness.

In any large organisation, there is a need for oversight and governance across all activities, and the PMO ensures alignment with corporate standards, so that risks are managed, and that control can be evidenced.

The PMO is the established source of organisational project culture, and this culture will change entirely with a move to agile. With the new ways of working, initiative control is the responsibility of the team. However, the PMO typically remains the custodian of the way the organisation professes to deliver projects, and as such, it will introduce a set of minimum standards, templates and controls in its role as the centre of excellence for solution delivery.

As such, it can act as a catalyst; identifying candidate projects for transition, assisting with risk management around dependencies and providing training and support for the new working practices.

Step 9 – Measure the Results Recipe

At the outset of the agile transformation, I recommended that the Enterprise Agile Coach should establish benchmark metrics that are appropriate for the organisational context. These benchmarks should provide a before and after comparison of the change. They also offer milestone like indications of the progression through the agile adoption journey as the capabilities identified on the transitional sundial.

Back to the PDCA cycle; the metrics provide actionable insight, helping the coach not only deliver value more quickly and reliably but also to relentlessly improve both team and organisational processes.

The Benefit of Measuring Recipe

Measuring the results keeps the focus on the intended strategic benefits from the agile transformation. Collecting and publishing the data from the agile teams and processes is half the challenge. Then using this information constructively to illustrate opportunities and success is essential.

Transformation Progress Recipe

What is the best way to get into the status of your transformation? Is a burndown chart the answer? Probably not! Could a scrum-style Sprint Review be suitable? I suspect only partially, most organisations, especially if they are geographically diverse, will want a status presentation in a form that they can circulate and use as a record.

Having a transformation sundial calibrates the activities in time, enabling rapid identification of progress status. In the transformation plan, conditions, namely statements of improved capability, are attached to time. The guardrails and success statements amplified the definition of the outcome. Collectively these should give binary indications of progress.

However, the reality with behavioural change activities is rarely binary and very often quite fuzzy! A summation of status is where narrative with sponsors comes into play *"individuals and interactions over processes and tools"*. It is often easier to establish and measure progress for the technical side of the agile transformation. The process change side can also be tested and data collected in terms of throughputs, operational risks and improvements. However, getting to the people side, the attitudinal or cultural change makes the difference and takes time is therefore much more complex to establish progress.

Measuring Progress Ingredients

As with all reporting, the Enterprise Agile Coach should ensure that any reports are concise and make use graphs where possible. Take the transformational sundial as an example and limit any formal reports to a single page. Of course, the formal report is not the only means of outward and possibly upwards communication. Successes and for that matter, some challenges should be shared via most communication channels.

Normalisation Stage – Moving to BAU

Normalisation is not an excuse for agile arrogance. We're fat happy and agile – we don't need to do any more. Not doing any more, is contrary to the Lean principle of relentless improvement, outlined in the first section of this book. Normalisation is the state where agile behaviours and practices become the organisational norm. Where continuous improvement is a natural process. Where plan do check act is everyday behaviour.

The Enterprise Agile Coach must consider switching to business-as-usual state, normalisation, as soon as is practical as few organisations will countenance a continuous transformation activity! Normalisation is not a step turned on overnight! Throughout the transformation process, the Enterprise Agile Coach's role is to organise training, set up the ecosystem and tools in transformation mode, to move into normalisation swiftly. Not all zones on the transformational sundial will progress at the same speed. So some aspects of the transformation may move into business-as-usual before others.

Activity Assurance and the PMO

In normalisation, the PMO as custodian of the methodologies also adopts a continuous improvement brief. They can also reinforce agile behaviours through their assurance remit.

Certain assurance functions expect to see documentation, plans, review points and, in fact, so do some project sponsors. When a team adopts an agile delivery methodology, these requirements do not change. It is just that the artefacts used are different.

Assurance is a fundamental responsibility of the PMO on behalf of Internal Audit. In undertaking this role, the PMO fulfils its obligations to internal stakeholders and, in some industries, also to the external regulatory bodies.

Assurance is profoundly different in the agile world, and it is a primary means by which the PMO adds value. While the following Project Assurance principles applied to an agile project or programme context, I have found they equally add value to organisations using traditional waterfall delivery processes.

The Activity Assurance Recipe

In undertaking project assurance in the Lean-Agile world, certain agile principles must be respected, namely:

- that the Agile team is self-managing;
- that Agile follows the "just enough" and "just in time" norms about documentation;
- that the team processes should be subject to continuous improvement;
- that working software is the primary illustration of progress.

An essential element of the assurance health check is that the activity is being reviewed and not the individuals.

Evaluating initiative health is largely a question of establishing if the project is likely to achieve the desired business outcomes. In an agile activity, documentation is a loose term and may include wall charts or a lightweight document. These statements are the essential kick-off declarations of intent and should exist on all projects. These outcomes or benefits were the reason why the organisation invested in the initiative. Care is needed to ensure that as the activity completes that the targeted benefits are not eroded. There are several different types of benefits, some financial others non-financial. In some activities, there will be a benefits realisation plan to manage. In others, the benefits will be realised by merely deploying the solution. With the agile focus on value delivered, every development team should have an excellent handle on its progress towards its business goal.

In evaluating the activity health, the assurance needs to establish the likelihood of achieving the targeted benefits.

Dinner Parties – Serving Suggestions

The transformational dinner party is where an Enterprise Agile Coach moves from a team to an organisational focus. Consequently, the challenges are bigger, but the rewards in terms of self-esteem are huge. Leading a team of agile coaches transitioning a large organisation from traditional to new ways of working is career-defining.

Like many business and non-business scenarios, success is dependent upon getting the basics right before starting to use individual flair and brilliance. The basics in the agile transformational space are:

- Conducting a thorough situational analysis.
- Preparing an outcome-based transformational plan or sundial.
- Communicating and listening then adapting the plan.
- Ensuring that you key focussed on the transformation goals and improvement metrics.
- Working your way out of a job because agile becomes business as usual.

References

[i] https://www.craiglarman.com/wiki/index.php?title=Larman%27s_Laws_of_Organisational_Behavior

[ii] Edgar H. Schein, Organisational Culture and Leadership, John Wiley & Sons, (2010)

[iii] Deming, W. Edwards, Out of the crisis. Cambridge, MA: Massachusetts Institute of Technology, (1986)

[iv] Kevin Forsberg and Harold Mooz, "The Relationship of System Engineering to the Project Cycle", in Proceedings of the First Annual Symposium of National Council on System Engineering, October 1991: 57 – 65.

[v] Ken Schwaber and Jeff Sutherland, The Scrum Guide, Scrum.org (2019) https://www.scrum.org/resources/scrum-guide.

[vi] David J. Anderson and Teodora Bozheva, Kanban Maturity Model: Evolving Fit-For-Purpose Organisations, (March 2018)

[vii] Ken Blanchard, Spencer Johnson, The One Minute Manager, William Morrow & Co, 1982

[viii] Imornefe Bowes and Robyn L. Jones, Working at the Edge of Chaos: Understanding Coaching as a Complex, Interpersonal System, The Sport Psychologist 2016

[ix] Whitmore, Sir John Coaching for performance: GROWing human potential and purpose: the principles and practice of coaching and leadership. People skills for professionals (4th ed.). Boston: Nicholas Brealey. (2009) [1992].

[x] Argyris, C. (1976). Increasing Leadership Effectiveness. New York: Wiley (1976)

[xi] Imornefe Bowes and Robyn L. Jones. Working at the Edge of Chaos: Understanding Coaching as a Complex, Interpersonal System, The Sport Psychologist, Volume 20: Issue 2, Pages: 235 – 245

[xii] Project Management Institute, Pulse of the Profession 2018 (2018)

[xiii] Tuckman, Bruce W. "Developmental sequence in small groups". Psychological Bulletin. 63 (6): 384 – 399, (1965)

[xiv] https://www.axelos.com/best-practice-solutions/msp/what-is-msp.

[xv] Bittner, Kurt; Spence, Ian. Use Case Modelling. Addison-Wesley Professional. ISBN 978-0-201-70913-1, 2008.

[xvi] Association of Project Managers, The Guide to Project Risk Analysis and Management, January 2018

[xvii] Association for Project Management (APM) Body of Knowledge, 7th Edition May 2019

[xviii] Tuckman, Bruce W. "Developmental sequence in small groups". Psychological Bulletin. 63 (6): 384 – 399, (1965)

[xix] Schwaber and Sutherland; The Scrum Guide, Scrum.org (2019) https://www.scrum.org/resources/scrum-guide.

[xx] Brooks Fred; The Mythical Man-Month: Essays on Software Engineering, Addison-Wesley, (1975)

[xxi] Tuckman, Bruce W. "Developmental sequence in small groups". Psychological Bulletin. 63 (6): 384 – 399, (1965)

[xxii] Ibid, Axelos, Managing Successful Programmes 4th Edition

[xxiii] Scott Ambler Adapting Agile Methods for Complex The Agile Scaling Model (ASM): Adapting Agile Methods for Complex Environments IBM 2009

[xxiv] Deming, W. Edwards, Out of the crisis. Cambridge, MA: Massachusetts Institute of Technology, 1986